ENGLISH POETRY
An Unfinished History

ENGLISH POETRY

An Unfinished History

By

JOHN DRINKWATER

With a Preface by
ST. JOHN ERVINE

BOOKS FOR LIBRARIES PRESS

FREEPORT, NEW YORK

First Published 1938
Reprinted 1971

INTERNATIONAL STANDARD BOOK NUMBER:
0-8369-5837-3

LIBRARY OF CONGRESS CATALOG CARD NUMBER:
74-160969

PRINTED IN THE UNITED STATES OF AMERICA

PREFACE

by ST. JOHN ERVINE

JOHN DRINKWATER, when he was within a few weeks of completing his fifty-fifth year, died in his sleep on 25 March 1937. This book, which deals with the matter most dear to his life, the art of poetry, was stopped in the middle of a sentence. Approaching the great figure of John Donne, the mystic poet and Dean of St. Paul's, Drinkwater noted down the unique quality of the divine—' he wrote like nobody else in his time, and nobody has written like him since, or ever will '—and then attempted to reveal Donne's secret; but he dropped his pen, we do not know why, before he had written one revelatory word, and in the night he died. Donne's secret may now be crystal clear to Drinkwater, revealed beyond a shadow of a doubt, but it remains, so far as this book is concerned, undisclosed. ' And the secret, so far as I can discover it, is that his thought . . .' That is the end. One might almost imagine that Donne had laid a bony finger on his hand and forbidden him to write another word.

Poetry was the chief and absorbing passion of John Drinkwater's life. Every line in this good book makes

v

the fact plain. Observe how lovingly he searches out some forgotten bard and brings back to life as much of him as can be restored. Corbet, ignored by *The Golden Treasury* and *The Oxford Book of English Verse*, shall not lie in neglect if John Drinkwater can help it. Robert Greene shall not continue in your knowledge merely as the irritable invalid who snarled at Shakespeare, but shall be shown as the author of a ' heavenly jingle ', and Thomas Carew, described in the *Dictionary of National Biography* as ' a man of dissipated habits ', shall be shown as something more : a poet who could write :

> Ask me no more where Jove bestows,
> When June is past, the fading rose ;
> For in your beauty's orient deep
> These flowers, as in these causes, sleep.

The habits, in Drinkwater's opinion, are not worth remembering : the poetry is. He takes care that poets whose names are nowhere recorded shall not be denied the honour of publication, and he rescues from forgotten miscellanies two lovely lyrics which are printed here on page 153.

How excellent a book this is. Here is a poet praising poets with skill and acumen, displaying his own preferences, yet denying grace to none who deserves it, even although the work may be little to his taste. There are spirit and wit in the judgements, surprisingly, perhaps, to those who supposed him to be devoid of a sense of humour ; and he deals shrewd blows to those curious persons who cannot believe that anything of any worth was written before they took hold of pens. 'Which of the new prophets', he pertinently demands, 'can explain how in any sense or at any time a host of golden daffodils is a less suitable theme for poetry than a blast-furnace?' Nor is he overpowered by great names, though he is never insolent to the mighty dead. Milton's contemptuous reference to rhyme is critically, but respectfully, examined and found wanting, nor can anyone doubt that Drinkwater has the better of the argument. With what civility he turns his attention to Mr. Eliot's verse, finding the good in it as faithfully as he finds the fault. I doubt if any discerning reader will lay down this book without feeling his knowledge and understanding of English poetry sensibly increased.

When I made friendship with him, he had already won great renown and fortune with his play, *Abraham Lincoln*, and was beginning to experience the blasts of envy which blow about a man who has committed the crime of success. I came to know him intimately, and I formed a great affection for him which was not diminished by the break in our encounters during the last year or two of his life. His detractors said of him that he was pompous, and they lost no opportunity of belittling his work, yet I never heard him say a single bitter word about his most implacable enemy. He had a natural resentment, but never once, in the years that I knew him, did I hear him belittle those who had belittled him. That was not his nature. He might complain of a man's criticism, but he did not complain of the man himself, nor did he, when angered by those who depreciated his work, attempt to revenge himself by depreciating theirs. He was incapable of anonymous assaults. That he had defects is indisputable, for he was a man and fallible like the rest of us, but meanness was not one of them, nor was spite. He was not envious of anyone's good fortune, but was eager to promote it. He leaves in my recollection the memory of a most generous nature and an affectionate and friendly disposition. His mind was cool and temperate, and he preserved that balance of belief which is essentially English. He was an *English* poet, not a *British* poet, and could not possibly have been mistaken for a man of any nationality but his own. In one of his poems, ' Water-meadows ', he reveals his attitude towards life in terms that identify him unmistakably to his friends :

Cool in the very furnace of July
The water-meadows lie ;
The green stalks of their grasses and their flowers
They still refresh at fountains never dry ;
And in the parchèd hours,
Taking the burning beams as a caress,
Perpetually watered, they defy
The sun's excess.

So let my mind be watered at the springs
Of temperate things ;
That when the fumes of passion, and the heat
Of intellectual pride
Menace my song, and threaten with defeat
The mood that lonely sings,
I may put all that vanity aside,

And keep my vision clear and cool as those
Good meadows, green
In the high summer day ;
May tell what bright ascensions I have seen,
To be no less attentive in repose,
And fresh in heart as they.

His generosity shines through these pages in which
appears a greater eagerness to praise than to dispraise,
not because their author is an unctuous flatterer who
turns a blind eye to faults in the hope that an eye no
less blind shall be turned to his, but because the best
that is in us appeals to him most. He had a gift for
friendship, and his friends will not forget him.

CONTENTS

I

DESIGN

IN 1922 it was my privilege to take some part in introducing the work of my friend, Edwin Arlington Robinson, to a wider circle of English readers than it had hitherto reached. Two years later, he wrote to me in a letter :

Speaking of poems, I am still in doubt as to whether you have ever been made to realize how deeply grateful I am to you for all your generous and disinterested efforts in the matter of my work. I hope so, for you may be sure that what you did was fully appreciated and will always be remembered. *Things go so fast nowadays, and there is so much less room than there used to be for the individual, that probably the most that any of us can hope for is that a few things may stick —and that is really hoping for a great deal.*

The words that I have italicized have a cardinal bearing upon the plan of this book. My personal opinion is that Robinson will take his place among the three or four major poets that America has so far produced. But he was also, as is usually the way with great poets, a very voluminous writer, producing a steady succession of poems that both by their length and by the toughness of their texture made exacting demands upon their readers. Indeed, he frequently expressed his surprise that so many people in America were willing to give them the requisite attention. 'I am still at a loss', he wrote of his *Tristram*, 'to understand how and why so many people have been able to read two hundred pages of blank verse, and apparently without much suffering, for I know just how such a thing looks. I have even walked by *Paradise Lost* without losing a train.'

Whatever claims his importance may make upon the future, therefore, he knew well enough that in the bewilderingly rapid accumulation of literature the bulk of his work could less and less hope for detailed consideration. There was really no melancholy in his misgiving. Being a poet, he was a realist, and quite content to face facts. His poetry was to himself a source of life-long satisfaction, self-expression richly and variously achieved, and it brought him much honour. That was well, and for the rest he hoped and asked no more than that in time to come 'a few things might stick'.

This book, then, is not a history of poetry in any academic sense. I use the word academic in admiration only. The critic who devotes many years to the resolution of a great poet's text, and leaves the workshop of Shakespeare or Milton or Wordsworth far tidier than he found it, must be honoured by all who care anything for the integrity of scholarship. Nor is there in the best of these men anything of dry-as-dust pedantry. I know from personal contact that they delight in the breath and finer spirit of the poetry that they so scrupulously anatomize. But theirs is only one of the methods of approach to poetry, and it has not been mine.

Neither does this book propose any such undertaking as W. J. Courthope's great History. In that, nothing that had been done in English poetry from first to last was to escape analysis. However widely individual taste may differ from Courthope's critical judgements, his story of English poetry down to the time of his conclusion is never likely to be more copiously or more authoritatively told. I can imagine no less alluring task than any such attempt.

The present design is rather to record the impression that English poetry has made upon a mind that for over thirty years has been engaged constantly under its influence and frequently in its practice. George Saintsbury, at once the most stupendous and the raciest of modern critics, once boasted wryly that he had read every published line of English poetry, good, bad and indifferent, and had enjoyed it all. In this at least I can approach if not seriously rival his eminence. I have read extensively in every poet of any consequence and in many of none. Beyond refreshing my memory and the selection of quotations, I have done no special reading for this book—that is a necessary part of the compact with myself. I wish to examine what poetry has meant to me as the natural habit of a lifetime, not as the intensive study for a set occasion. And my concern here is with the poetry alone. There will, for example, be but little biographical reference, save in so far as it may throw some light on the continuity of my narrative. Nor will there be more than casual allusions to the opinions about poetry that have been expressed by other people. A plain text of the poets, and thirty years of contemplation on the life therein embodied—that is the equipment to which I propose to confine myself.

In such a scheme certain defects are probable, perhaps inevitable. But they do not affect the fundamentals of the design ; I would even claim that in respect of it

they are not defects at all. First, there is the question
of scholarship. On this matter I may use words that
I wrote some years ago in reviewing W. H. C. Davis's
wise and brilliant study of *The Age of Grey and Peel*.

He makes not the smallest parade of his scholarship, but
we leave his book with a profound impression that what
he don't know isn't knowledge. And yet, it is at this
point that certain obstinate questionings intrude upon our
admiration.

What precisely is the value of knowledge in itself? To
this question it would seem that a consideration of language
affords us at least a partial answer. For example, suppose
a linguist of to-day to rediscover with demonstrable cer-
tainty the speech of the Cretan peasants of the classic age,
and of the Saxon serfs who followed Harold to Hastings.
He will probably be esteemed as a scholar. To this know-
ledge he may further add an intimacy with a dozen other
dead tongues that were once the daily speech of the common
people. By such a process he may attain international
eminence. And yet, on reflection, we realize that his dis-
tinction is but to know imperfectly what was once known
perfectly by great numbers of uneducated and illiterate
persons . . .

Here is Professor Davis with a comprehensive and, we
are sure, a perfectly reliable fund of information about every
kind of social activity in the period of which he is writing.
He can, for instance, give a very rapid chronicle of the
popular societies which in the last decade of the eighteenth
century were exploring means of reform and advocating
their views with varying degrees of vehemence. He can
relate these organizations one to the other ; he has their
respective programmes and their methods of activity and
the views of their leaders at his finger-tips. But here, again,
we cannot help remembering that all these things were once
within the knowledge of poor weavers and chainmakers,
who could do no more than put marks to their names, and

whose political consciousness was at the mercy of any sharp-witted demagogue who chose to exploit it. So that knowledge in itself does not appear to be a very notable thing ; the most we can say is that it needs special gifts for a scholar like Professor Davis to acquire what was once a condition of the uninstructed mind.

These reflections are strictly relevant to the textual criticism of poetry. The removal of corruptions from a poet's text is a laudable, though sometimes a hazardous, enterprise. It will hardly be disputed, however, that the reader of a poet before this salutary process has taken place is at no appreciable disadvantage in his approach to the essential life and presiding imagination of the poet's work as against the reader who comes to it in the light of the latest scholarship. So sensitive and liberal a scholar as Ernest de Selincourt, for example, whose work on Wordsworth is a model of what such research should be, would not claim a closer contact with the poetry of Wordsworth than was possible to Matthew Arnold. And if the kitchen-maid at Rydal Mount—there was, I think, no kitchen-maid at Dove Cottage—ever heard her master read his poems, or was even curious to look at his manuscripts, then there were points within her simple knowledge that challenge the most careful investigations of highly trained scholarship to-day.

Saintsbury himself was notoriously careless of these things. Many a fastidious Oxford soul has been deeply and genuinely shocked when confronted with the errors in that magnificent assembling, the *Minor Poets of the Caroline Period*. But it is not to condone Saintsbury's occasional slovenliness to say that no critic in recent times has brought a finer zest, a surer taste, or a more penetrating sympathy to the reading of poetry than he. I shall look impenitently to his ghost if any one should upbraid me for lapses from the stricter accuracy.

There is, further, the question of personal preferences : likes and dislikes for which there is scarcely any logical accounting. That poetry is a greater thing than any poet is a useful platitude to keep in mind. The pursuit of comprehensive knowledge in any subject is an attractive occupation. Caring for poetry, we justly wish to know all we can about every possible poet and his work. But the essential virtue communicable to us from poetry is something much more definable, or if not more definable, more fixed, in compass. There is a limit to the stimulus and refreshment that each mind is capable of receiving from this source. Some minds, though I suspect that they are rare, may be insusceptible to poetry altogether ; others may find their capacities exhausted by a casual acquaintance with *The Golden Treasury* ; others again may range all the pastures of poetry without surfeit. Even the most extensive reader, however, is likely to find some poets who, although good, are not within the scope of his necessity. He may enjoy them, but he could do without them ; his delight in and profit from poetry would not have been substantially less if he had never met them.

It has been so in my own experience. Choosing names at a hazard, my life would have been incalculably the poorer without Chaucer, Shakespeare, Milton, Marvell, Wordsworth, Keats, Arnold. To them and a score of others I return again and again in my thought. But Spenser, Donne, Dryden, Collins, Landor, Rossetti, for some reason mean less to me. I have enjoyed them, sometimes excitedly, and I know that in general they belong to the rank of those others. Nevertheless, poetry without them would still for me have been much

what it is. Reservations obviously have to be made
in respect of many starry points in Spenser, half a dozen
supreme lines of satire in Dryden, and a few pages of
lyrics by the others all told. It is of their work as a
whole that I speak. I have read *Paradise Lost* perhaps
ten times ; I could not in strict honour say that I had
read *The Fäerie Queen* once.

In my attempt to describe what poetry has meant
to me, therefore, I shall ask for the friendly indulgence
of readers who may find that my illustrations are drawn
too freely from poets whom they themselves do not
chiefly affect, while others that they do are relatively
neglected. I trust that no important figure in English
poetry will altogether escape my notice, as certainly
none has escaped my gratitude, but my intention through-
out will be rather to project a living image of my own
experience of that poetry as a single cumulative achieve-
ment of the race, than to compile an exact chronicle of
the poets who have made it. And since this is a con-
fessional, the first person singular will be a necessarily
recurrent figure.

II

THE NATURE AND FUNCTION OF POETRY

IN asserting that poetry more than anything else in life has for me stimulated the imagination and helped to make anxiety tolerable, it is necessary at the outset to explain my conception of poetry and to define the virtue for which I look to it. In passing it may be said that these general considerations could in principle be applied to other arts, music for example, from which other people may derive the satisfaction that poetry has been to me.

All doctrine is dangerous, but in a discussion such as this certain axiomatic premises must be laid down. And first this : the difference between poetry and all other forms of literary expression is so pronounced that it may almost be called generic. In the exercise of creative energy there comes a moment when suddenly the material that is being wrought passes into a state of incandescence, and is transmuted into something new and strange. The origin of this process defies the speculations of philosophy, but no one who has experienced it has any doubt as to its burning actuality. The excitement of writing poetry is comparable to that of no other form of literary creation. Much sentimental rubbish has been talked about inspiration, but

8

that does not make the phenomena of inspiration any the less impressive in itself. When a good poem is being written, something is happening beyond the ordaining of the poet's common faculties. Words and images are evoked from deeps that he has never consciously explored, idea is fused with idea by an alchemy over which he has no deliberate control, and unthought-of associations announce themselves in a serene and inevitable lucidity. And all the time this marvel of expression is related, more or less patently as the case may be, to the common experience of life. The poet is the most uncompromising of realists, but his poem is reality transfigured.

With certain majestic passages of prose in mind, it cannot be asserted out of hand that the apocalyptic speech of poetry must of necessity assume the metrical pattern of verse, but the fact is that it almost invariably does so. The exalted mood of poetry turns naturally to the formal rhythms of verse that have been beating in the minds of men back through the ages. Difficult as this may be to explain, it is impossible to explain it away. For the practical purposes of discussion, poetry and verse, while they are not synonymous, may be taken to be inseparable, and when I speak of poetry the vehicle of verse is implied.

Poetry, then, is life purified. Not purified, indeed, of sorrow or even of shame, but purified of insignificance. Some central power and purpose in the poet projects him into a region of undistracted vision, and there he sees truth with an absolute clarity that is beyond the reach of thought. In the moment of this realization, and in the moment only, he perfects his own being. Creation once achieved, the supreme felicity passes, never by that particular achievement to be recaptured.

It is the act or condition of vision rather than the thing seen that counts, that makes poetry the wonder it is. A good poem may be written *about* anything, a fact which in my view reduces much recent critical writing to futility. There is a suggestion among the poets, many of them highly gifted, who have followed Mr. T. S. Eliot, that poetry, in its obligations to represent or interpret its own age, should to-day discard the cows and haystacks of the neo-Georgians and concentrate on the more virile aspects of aviation and cantilever bridges. Communism and fascism, it seems, are also calling. Even if we accept this rather childish misrepresentation of the Georgian material, which of the new prophets can explain how in any sense or at any time a host of golden daffodils is a less suitable theme for poetry than a blast-furnace ? The question is now, as it always has been and always must be, what sort of a poem has the poet made of either ? In terms of poetry, modern machinery is no more significant of life than a primrose or a milk-pail, whatever it may be in the sphere of social or political propaganda.

On the contrary, if it comes to that, the primrose preceded the motor-car and is likely to survive it. Further, it might be said empirically that poetry is instinctively inclined to a preoccupation with things of basic decency, and that the modern mechanization of society is associated with much that is destructive and demoralizing. These considerations, however, need not be pressed. If an automatic road-breaker or the collapse of the gold standard be the occasion of good poems, their poets are justified. But it is a radical error to suppose that these and all such manifestations are opening up a new world to which poetry has hitherto had no access. Of themselves, they are but fugitive disturbances upon the surface of the life from which poetry has always drawn its material. *The Waste Land* may be aware of social conditions that were unknown to Wordsworth and Thomas Hardy, but in no essential respect is it a more modern poem than *The Prelude* or *The Dynasts* ; which is not to infer that, remarkable as it may be, it is to be ranked with either.

We are brought back to the trite assertion that poetry is primarily and immutably concerned with the emotions that do not change in a changing world. But truth, however trite, needs ever new witnesses, and to be afraid of saying what may be obvious is a meaner kind of cowardice than to be afraid of saying what may be unpopular. Poetry takes no stock of fashions, has no vocation to be up to date. For many people, that is poetry's disqualification. They think that poetry is therefore indifferent to the problems and movements of reality. To others it is poetry's supreme vindication. They see in poetry, because of this circumstance, the one sure escape from delusion into the security of abiding beauty, which Keats recorded as the only truth.

So much, in brief, for the nature of poetry. What, then, of its function, of its use in the world after it has served the poet's own imperative need ? Or, to become strictly personal again, of what does the satisfaction that I have derived from poetry consist ? It is hardly enough to say that in reading poetry we capture something of the poet's own delight at the moment of creation. In a sense this is true, but it is not the whole truth. The reflection, however faint it may be, of the poet's ecstatic moment in our own minds is his unconditional gift to us, and a noble one it is. But to see the matter in that light and that light only is to imply a passivity on the part of the reader that does less than justice to his share in the transaction. For the reading of poetry is a collaboration between poet and reader to which each contributes spiritual activity in his own degree.

Questions of physical health apart, our conception of perfect well-being is conditioned by the ideal of a complete orderliness of mind. A mind that is wholly in control and master of the experience upon which it works is, within the scope of human limitations, a happy mind. Accepting the logical issues of this view, we shall find that, so long as the given condition of mind is preserved, the satisfaction can be independent of the nature of the experience to which the mind is directed. Strictly speaking, a mind, granted this complete and determining control, can be happy even in the contemplation of material misfortune. Ideally, this would be true, sometimes indeed may be true in actual experience, even when the misfortune is being suffered by the personality of the particular mind itself. Our conception of God is not of a being who is either insensible of or indifferent to the wrongs and miseries of the world that He has created, but neither is it of one who is desolated by these. It is, rather, of one who perceiving all with absolute vision, finds in all, in what we call good and in what we call evil alike, an equal satisfaction, serene in the knowledge that what to us appears insoluble will be resolved. The universal mind, or God, accepts evil as readily as good because it is equally master of both. Indeed, it may be that the mastery, the defeat, of evil is to the infinitely capable and disciplined mind a deeper delight even than the perfect contemplation of good. This possibility is supported by our own human delight in great tragic art, which is, perhaps, the most exquisite form of aesthetic appreciation of which we are capable. As I say, it is ideally possible for us to be happy in the contemplation of our own misfortunes, though the ideal is rarely if ever attainable to human imperfection. Once, however, the personal consideration is removed, there is no question as to our delight in perfectly apprehended tragedy. In witnessing tragic drama, we participate in the event at the poet's bidding, and, in the word of antiquity, our spirits are purged when, passing through the catastrophe, we find that the foundations of life are unshaken, that even heroic disaster is powerless to destroy us, that we have defeated evil.

Practical daily life, however, is not governed by these ideal conditions. In its conduct we are continually beset by circumstance, often apparently accidental in character, that confuses vision and makes the orderly control of experience almost impossible. We have some reason for believing that never has the life of the individual been so disorganized by the conditions of society as it is to-day, but, however that may be, man in the ordinary conduct of his affairs has always had to contend with distractions that blur the sharp edges of significance, and deny him the steady realization of serene vision. From this state of bondage he is for ever seeking escape. That may be accepted as a universal condition of the human mind—it is striving always towards emancipation from the fetters that hold it fast in a world of plaguing distortion, of distempers not grave in themselves but impeding the clear currents of thought, of trifling vexations that are yet serious enough to upset the steady balance without which it cannot possess the peace of understanding.

Most people in these conditions turn to what is called

recreation for relief.   Sports and games, the more super-
ficial forms of entertainment, hobbies and holiday travel,
owe their popularity to the common wish for any change
of occupation as an escape from the strain of anxieties
that perplex the ordinary routine.   Recreation in this
sense has lost most of its literal meaning.   People so
employed are finding not so much true re-creation as
a momentary rest from burdens.   The refreshment is
necessary, but limited in its operation.   From it we go
back to the routine not with heightened energy, but
with the old energy repaired.   We are not better
instruments than we were before, we are merely no
worse.   The appeal to poetry is made with a larger
hope.

In my own experience, the appeal may not be made
at the actual times when the misfortunes or the vexa-
tions are chiefly operative.   If I want to get my mind
off some immediate anxiety, it is not to poetry that I
turn, but to Wimbledon, or detective fiction, or English
stoneware, or a cross-word puzzle.   For the approach
to poetry the mood has to be relatively tranquil.   But
once the approach is successfully made, the effect pro-
duced differs in kind from that of all those diversions.
Wimbledon and such are pleasant and wholesome
narcotics, but no more.   When, however, with a
mind well disposed for the adventure, I find myself
reading—

> The grave's a fine and private place,
> But none I think do there embrace . . .

or

> the self-same song that found a path
> Through the sad heart of Ruth, when, sick for home,
> She stood in tears amid the alien corn . . .

or

> The hare is running races in her mirth;
> And with her feet she from the plashy earth
> Raises a mist; that, glittering in the sun
> Runs with her all the way, wherever she doth run . . .

or

> Nothing is here for tears, nothing to wail
> Or knock the breast, no weakness, no contempt,
> Dispraise, or blame, nothing but well and fair,
> And what may quiet us in a death so noble . . .

then my mind is stimulated to a lasting enrichment of its powers. It is not only that in this inspiration of words an experience has been imparted that is new in its own particular; beyond that, and even more radically important to me, my capacity for experiencing, for perceiving, has been permanently enlarged by this particular act of experience or vision, my faculties have been permanently sharpened, and my mind goes back to its routine avocations with a surer mastery than it employed before. This, as I see it, is the function of poetry in its relation to the reader.

III

POETRY AND PROSE

THE passages from Marvell, Keats, Wordsworth and Milton, quoted in the preceding chapter, are of immediately striking beauty, magical at once and for ever in their incantation. They assert themselves as being among the chief felicities of the great poems in which they occur, poems that, however sure they may be in their movement, cannot and do not achieve this happy excellence all the time. Marvell's poem *To His Coy Mistress* also contains :

> And while thy willing Soul transpires
> At every pore with instant fires . . .

Even the perfect *Ode to a Nightingale* touches the relative flatness of

> Adieu ! the fancy cannot cheat so well
> As she is fam'd to do, deceiving elf . . .

while *Resolution and Independence* has—

> And now a stranger's privilege I took ;
> And drawing to his side, to him did say,
> ' This morning gives us promise of a glorious day . . .'

16

and *Samson Agonistes* :

> Some dismal accident it needs must be ;
> What shall we do, stay here or run and see ?

These lines, even the least inspired of them, are suitable to their context, but it is manifest as soon as we read them that in themselves they have nothing of the creative passion that informs those others. Two questions follow. First, has a poem in its entirety an essential value greater than that of its most clearly inspired passages ? And second, in what, if any, way does a poem that only intermittently reaches the high levels of poetry excel a work of sustained imaginative prose ?

The first question may be considered with reference to the *Ode to a Nightingale* and *Resolution and Independence*. In the first of the poems, to be sure, it asks itself less pertinently than is common even in the case of masterpieces of under a hundred lines in length. Keats here obeys his own injunction to Shelley to fill every rift with ore, his high invention hardly faltering from first to last. Not half a dozen lines in the eight stanzas fall even to the questionable level of ' deceiving elf '.

The whole poem is incandescent, and no parts of it can be regarded as pensioners on the rest. Wordsworth's poem about the leech-gatherer is on another footing, and throws our question into sharp relief. It is impossible to make a prose transcript of the Nightingale ode without losing the essential significance of the poem entirely. That resides in the poetic revelation that is sustained phrase by phrase from the first line to the last. Of Wordsworth's poem, on the other hand, a brief transcript might be made that would not wholly do violence to the content matter of the original. On a bright spring morning after a storm, the poet is wandering on the moor, rejoicing in the general gladness. Suddenly and unaccountably he falls into dejection, and in this mood he meets an old man gathering leeches from a pond, who tells him that although things in the leech business are not what they used to be, he still perseveres and manages to maintain himself. Deeply impressed by the old man's resolution and independence, the poet pulls himself together, and determines in the future when he is tempted to misgivings and self-doubt to remember the leech-gatherer.

That is not Wordsworth's poem, but it is a reasonably faithful account of what it is about. In transmuting this material into poetry, Wordsworth frequently achieves beauties comparable to the image of the hare running through the wet grass. In the intervals between these, however, there are passages of a definitely lowered pressure, and this even when allowance has been made for the poet's sometimes rather constrained observation of his own celebrated doctrine that poetry should approximate to the language of common speech. Such passages in this poem have the merit always of being clear and to the point, and they can hardly ever be said to fall into the banality of which Wordsworth was occasionally capable. Nevertheless, the high poetic discovery is intermittent.

> A gentle answer did the old man make,
> In courteous speech which forth he slowly drew :
> And him with further words I thus bespake,
> ' What occupation do you there pursue ?
> This is a lonesome place for one like you . . . '

That takes its place fitly enough in the poem, but in itself it can hardly claim to be notable poetry. It may be doubted whether even the metrical movement gives

it any value above that of a prose statement. Is such
a passage, then, in terms of poetry a dead weight in the
poem, and if so does it follow that in most poems, since
what is true of *Resolution and Independence* is true of most
excellent poems of a like length, we can only look for
the pure communication of poetry at irregular intervals ?
The answer to the latter part of this question must
seem to be that it is so. In reading Wordsworth's
poem, we feel the apocalyptic touch often, but not
steadily throughout the narrative. The moral implica-
tions from which the material of the poem is gathered
are pleasing to reflection, but they do not liberate the
shaping powers of the imagination. The narrative itself,
admirably told, is of a character to engage without
deeply stirring the mind. Story and moral alike have
a literal meaning that, detached from the organic life
of the poem, have not the transforming virtue of poetry,
whatever their merits otherwise may be. And yet
without these elements the poem could not exist. The
poet, having selected them for his purpose, sets his
creative faculty to work on them ; and the result is
instructive to our problem. The basic material remains
a simple statement, but the poet's perception of it is
so intense that he irradiates the argument with frequent
images and phrases that are not only inspired themselves,
but shed an illumination over the whole poem, so that
passages that in detachment have no more than the
value of prose statement borrow a poetic life from the
visionary heights by which they are enclosed. ' And
all the air is filled with pleasant noise of waters ', the
hare in the grass, the cloud that ' moveth all together,
if it move at all ', the ' mighty Poets in their misery
dead ', these and other such moments have an informing
power that permeates the other parts of the poem, and

draws the story and moral into an organic life that transcends their prose nature. Once the poem as a whole, in fact, has been received by the mind, we find it impossible any longer to make that detachment of the less urgent parts from the rest. They still do not communicate to us the excitement of the great moments, but they cannot be regarded as dead weight. Once we have realized them in the true perspectives of the completed work, they do not impair our poetical satisfaction in the whole. On the contrary, they augment it. For just as in themselves, if we can so consider them, they fall short of revelation, so also are they conditions out of which the unimpeachable moments of revelation spring. Isolate the great images and phrases from their humbler context, and they too lose half their virtue. So forcibly is this the case, that sometimes a whole poem may become memorable by the saving grace of one such life-giving line. Edward Dyer's ' My mind to me a kingdom is ' is a beautiful poem, but its fifty lines would suffer irreparable loss without the first from which it takes its name.

Our second question may be considered by way of *Paradise Lost* and Thomas Hardy's *Mayor of Casterbridge*. I choose these examples because the former is secure against any rivalry among the great long poems in the language, magnificent as that rivalry is in two or three instances, and because Thomas Hardy gives me greater pleasure than any other writer of prose narrative. Although the sustained splendour of *Paradise Lost* is fresh matter for astonishment every time we return to it, there are inevitably many passages in the twelve books of the epic where the high invention flags, or the necessities of the narrative enforce a lowering of the poetic pressure. *The Mayor of Casterbridge*, conversely, is

especially notable among the great English novels for
the intense vitality of its detail, its almost complete
emancipation from superfluous tissue. In this respect,
indeed, it is more remarkable even than Milton's poem.
In some others, it reaches high, perhaps it may be said
the highest imaginative excellence. In shape it has a
tragic perfection that the Greek dramatists would have
acknowledged. The human emotion is sublime at once
in its penetration and its simplicity, and the scene of
the narrative is presented with a passion that imparts
living significance to a tent at a country fair, a corn-
factor's loft, the windows of a house, a forsaken earth-
works. Here, again, it may plausibly be argued that
the substance of the novel, to our modern minds at
any rate, makes a directer appeal than that of the poem.
And yet, *Paradise Lost* remains a greater work of art
than *The Mayor of Casterbridge* (the same thing might
be said of Hardy's own *Dynasts*). Why?

In making the comparison for the purpose of estab-
lishing a general principle, one must be careful to avoid
any seeming disparagement of a particular work. *The
Mayor of Casterbridge* could not conceivably be more
admirable than it is, and I for one certainly could not
admire it more. Nor is Hardy any less surely master
of his material than Milton in the works cited. When
an artist achieves his creative intention perfectly, as
Hardy does in this story, it is graceless to complain that
he has not succeeded in some other aim, and the con-
tention that *The Mayor of Casterbridge* is a lesser feat
of creative energy than *Paradise Lost* is made only by
way of discovering in what way a supreme masterpiece
of poetry is greater than a supreme masterpiece of prose.

In the works under consideration, Milton and Hardy
may be allowed to be equally masters of their material;

3

the difference lies in the nature of the material mastered. At least, it is from this point that we must set out on our search for the solution of our problem. Superficially, Milton's material has an appearance of being sublimer, more cosmic in character, than Hardy's ; but superficially only. On examination, the homely Wessex life of Hardy's novel is found to be as deeply rooted in what our human perception takes to be eternal verity as the heavenly hierarchies of Milton's poem. Henchard frustrated in the social currents of Casterbridge is as elemental a figure as Satan brooding over the chaos of his defeat. But the contemplation of his Wessex chronicle does not affect Hardy in the same way as the contemplation of heaven and hell affects Milton. In his Preface to *Jude the Obscure*, Hardy wrote : ' Like former productions of this pen, *Jude the Obscure* is simply an endeavour to give shape and coherence to a series of seemings, or personal impressions, the question of their consistency or their discordance, of their permanence or their transitoriness, being regarded as not of the first moment.' What Hardy proposes to himself is to scrutinize the events of his creative experience, concentrating on his ' personal impressions ' of phenomena, and implicitly allowing the durable significance to look after itself. There is a certain cool deliberateness in the artist's approach to his material. Once he is engaged with it, the creative temperature rises, often to a fine passion, and durable significance is established securely enough. Perhaps no work of its time has dated in the bad sense so little as Hardy's. Even so slight and apparently unsophisticated a tale as *Under the Greenwood Tree* is as fresh and convincing to-day as when it was written over sixty years ago. And yet in all the beautiful contriving of the Wessex novels this condition remains :

in the mastery is a slightly ironic awareness of itself,
the creator controlling his material with the superb
assurance of a potter at the wheel. This, it may be said,
and said fairly, is true of any great artistic creation, but
although this is so a difference is still to be found between
the shaping disposition of one creative act and another.
In saying that Hardy's control of his material is cool or
deliberate, no suggestion is made that thereby he fails to
draw everything out of the material that it is capable
of yielding, or that in any way he retards its own self-
fertilizing processes. It is only that, while passion may
result freely from the creative exercise, the creative
mood is not primarily dominated by passion at the
outset. The distinction is a fine one, and, indeed,
asserts itself only when we contrast the creative origins
of such a work as *The Mayor of Casterbridge* with those
of such a work as *Paradise Lost*. Then we perceive that
although the originating impulse in Hardy is grand
enough to achieve the highest possible success in his
design, there is still an important difference between
it and the originating impulse of *Paradise Lost*.

At the opening of his epic Milton writes :

And chiefly Thou O Spirit, that dost prefer
Before all Temples th'upright heart, and pure,
Instruct me, for Thou know'st ; Thou from the first
Wast present, and with mighty wings outspread
Dove-like satst brooding on the vast Abyss
And mad'st it pregnant : What in me is dark
Illumine, what is low raise and support ;
That to the height of this great Argument
I may assert Eternal Providence,
And justify the ways of God to men.

There at once we have it. ' What in me is dark illumine,
what is low raise and support.' Never was poet's soul

stirred by a prouder or more passionate humility than Milton's at that moment, but the spirit of humility itself was profoundly significant to the contract. There is here a sense of dedication, of ecstatic surrender to the purpose in hand, that invest the creation with passion from the start. Everything that follows in the mighty poem is true to this conceiving mood. As we delight in Hardy's mastery, we are conscious of a perfect manipulation of material at the master's will. As we delight in Milton's, we are conscious of this too, but with a difference. We are aware now of some spirit of instruction on which the poet and we alike are waiting expectantly, such as communicates with us in the fastnesses of the woods and hills. There is a sense of frustration in the mysterious contact, only of something greater than the daily stature of our mortality. In Hardy's work we feel that everything possible to be said about the matter is said with a lovely finality. In Milton's we feel that in a vision as intense and far-ranging as ever has been given to man, we are yet waiting on discovery. The poet's comprehension is splendidly equal to every demand made upon it, but it is in that mood of prayer, of dedication, of humility, that the revelation is won. It is this that gives the whole work a grandeur, an exhilaration above even the imperishable excellence of Hardy's narrative. It is this, too, that impels the poet to the majestic yet infinitely tender harmonies of his verse, from which we derive a sensuous, it may almost be said actually a physical, pleasure that is beyond the compass of prose. To read *The Mayor of Casterbridge* is to rejoice in the wonder of man's invention ; to read *Paradise Lost* is, keeping a firm hold on our human experience, to sing with the morning stars.

IV

READING POETRY

A SMALL practical problem that arises in our approach to poetry is that of the best way to read it. If we dogmatize at all here, it must be very delicately, since every sensible reader will form a habit best suited to his own taste, but a few general observations on the question may not be out of place.

Just as among the literary arts poetry shows the highest degree of concentration, so the reading of poetry calls for an attention not demanded by the literature legitimately designed for the amusement of tired minds. Contact with poetry, if it is to be vital, needs the exercise of our faculties at their best. This is not to say that poetry is to be regarded as something ceremonial and difficult. The teaching of poetry in the schools has in the past been largely ineffective because of this error. Such teaching of poetry is in any case to some extent embarrassed by the necessity of conforming to fixed hours, which often may not conform with the mood of the pupil. It is well enough in general principle that a young person at school should have to do what he is told, and fall in with the scheduled routine of work ; well enough, that is, with the possible exception of so chancy a matter as the appreciation of poetry.

Clearly, however, there is no practical way of avoiding this necessity, and the teacher's obligation is thereby all the greater to avoid any tedious formality in his instruction. Failure in this has endued many thousands of young minds with an aversion to poetry from which they have never recovered. On the other hand, the teaching of poetry in schools is by all means to be encouraged, since there are very few young minds which are not susceptible to the appeal of poetry if properly guided. It is the teacher's problem to strike the balance nicely between making the study of poetry a pleasure, and making it at the same time something that cannot be undertaken irresponsibly.

The maturer mind, that can choose its own occasions, will find that poetry does not readily disclose her secrets to moods of haste or exhaustion. The reviewing of poetry in the press, of which in past years I have myself done perhaps more than my share, is mostly carried on in conditions that are fair neither to the poets nor the reviewers nor the readers of the journals. The only just and satisfactory way of noticing a new book of poems would be to send it to a competent and unprejudiced judge, leaving its consideration indefinitely to his leisure and inclination. The critic who has to write an article about half a dozen new books of poems by Monday week is nine times out of ten in a position of hopeless inadequacy, however little he may know it. Assuming the books to have some merit, the odds are all against his being able in the prescribed time to make and relate any interesting discovery of it. Indeed, an *ad hoc* assertion may be made that nobody in any case can read six books of poems on end with any justice either to the poet's vision or his own intelligence.

My own experience is that even when the mood is

right, poetry cannot profitably be read for a long continuous period of time. I find, in the most favourable circumstances, an hour or so of any poet enough at a sitting. After that symptoms of strain, of labour, begin to appear, and the finer zest of communication shows signs of wear. It is time to stop. And, more often, ten minutes is nearer the mark than an hour. Poetry should never be read when the attention is fixed only by deliberate effort. True, the right reading of poetry demands the maximum effort of which our mind and imagination are capable, but that maximum operates only when we are not conscious of it as effort at all.

This demand for intentness in reading poetry does not imply that poetry itself is generally or even often obscure in its material meaning. In the practice of the poets there is no rule about this. To take, for example, four poets of one age, working in the same intellectual environment. Tennyson and Arnold are scarcely ever abstruse in thought while Browning and Meredith constantly are. Tennyson and Arnold are not in consequence either more or less subtle or profound than the others. The clear nostalgia of *The Scholar Gipsy* and the complex psychological curiosity of *The Ring and the Book* have in themselves an equal significance as material for poetry. The intellectual structure of a poem may be simple or involved at the poet's will. The obscurity, if it is there, must, however, be in the material and never in the expression. Obscure expression is no expression at all. At the same time, when the poet gives clear expression to involved thought, it does not follow that the thought is immediately apparent to the reader. Browning frequently says something quite plainly and yet leaves us perplexed for a time as to what precisely that something is. Writing of this

kind is not fundamentally obscure.   The most damaging
thing that can be said of it is that many readers reason-
ably enough will not be bothered to make the effort
of discovering what it is about.   For it is not the close
attention of a fresh and vigorous mind that is required
here, but a particular sort of mental ingenuity to which
some intelligent people are inclined and others not.

> The space
> Of time we judge so meagre to embrace
> The Parts, were more than plenty, once attained
> The whole, to quite exhaust it : for nought's gained
> But leave to look—not leave to do : Beneath
> Soon sates the looker—look Above, then ! Death
> Tempts ere a tithe of Life be tasted. Live
> First, and die soon enough, Sordello ! Give
> Body and spirit the bare right they claim
> To pasture thee on a voluptuous shame . . .

Browning here does not falter in expression.   He knows
exactly what he means and exactly says it.   The evident
stamp of mastery is on his words.   But the reader who
gives up the pursuit of the poet's thought may be ab-
solved from the charge of an indifference to poetry.
Poetry is here for our apprehension, but something else
is here too which in our readiness for poetry we may
not be disposed to apprehend.

When, on the other hand, the thought of a poem
is immediately manifest to our understanding, we none
the less need the highest exercise of our perceptive
faculties to apprehend the poetry.

> And now 'twas like all instruments,
> Now like a lovely flute ;
> And now it is an angel's song,
> That makes the heavens be mute.

It ceased ; yet still the sails made on
A pleasant noise till noon,
A noise like of a hidden brook
In the leafy month of June,
That to the sleeping woods all night
Singeth a quiet tune.

The meaning of that is as immediately plain as it would
be if Coleridge had said ' I'm cold ', or ' It's four o'clock
in the afternoon '. Browning's meaning in that passage
from *Sordello*, it may be added, is no less plain, when
we have found it. In allowing that Browning's mean-
ing is difficult to perceive, we must be careful not to
assume that there is any doubt as to what it is once
it is perceived. A poet cannot rightly be censured for
making us search closely for his meaning at all, but he
can if he leaves us debating as to whether he means one
thing or another. Extreme agility of thought is not
inconsistent with poetry ; confusion of thought is.
While, however, there certainly is neither in the lines
from *The Ancient Mariner*, the poetry that invests the
pure limpidity of thought still communicates its full
life only to our intentest mood. Which is another
way of saying that the thought or material meaning
of Coleridge's lines, simple as it appears, has by the
transmutation of poetry become as significant as the
intellectual complication of Browning's.

The actual transmutation of his thought and feeling
into poetry is achieved by the poet by means of his
expression, his words. Whether the material be by
nature simple or complex, the expression above all else
must be clear in the sense of not being confused. The
Sordello lines are difficult, but they are clear. That
they are not so to our instant understanding is beside
the point ; what is necessary is that they should be

clear in terms of the poet's purpose, which is expression of his thought, and this they are. They have at once the air of authority about them which proclaims that the poet has found the shape he sought, and in that the essential claims of clarity are satisfied.

The provision that poetry must be clear in expression is, however, not quite so simple as it sounds. The question has been much investigated by poets and critics, but Aristotle said the first word of consequence upon it, and we should not be far wrong if we added that he said the last.

The merit of diction [he wrote] is to be clear and not commonplace. The clearest diction is that made up of ordinary words, but it is commonplace . . . That which employs unfamiliar words is dignified and outside the common usage . . . But if a poet writes entirely in such words, the result will be . . . jargon. We need then a sort of mixture of the two. For the one kind will save the diction from being prosaic and commonplace . . . whereas the ordinary words give clarity.

Any treatise on the diction of poetry, and it is an inexhaustible theme, can but be an elaboration of this cardinal text.

One elaboration only shall be ventured here. The use of the rare, Aristotle's ' unfamiliar ' word, is a device of manifest credentials in poetry.

> Golden lads and lasses must,
> As *chimney-sweepers*, come to dust,

and

> To build *a new Jerusalem*
> In England's green and pleasant land,

and

> Life, *like a dome of many-coloured glass*
> Stains the white radiance of Eternity,

and

> Still nursing the unconquerable hope,
> Still *clutching the inviolable shade,*

such examples, which can be endlessly matched in English poetry, show the use of the 'unfamiliar' word clearly in operation. Since the time of Wordsworth, and particularly in quite recent years, the term 'poetic diction' has been used freely to denote a kind of false inflation of language, the trivial employment of ready-made figures and phrases by versifiers who borrow from the common stock without enriching it. But that 'poetic diction' has commonly been made to mean 'bad poetic diction' is no reason why criticism should be deprived of the term in its proper sense. The passages given above are instances of poetic diction that cannot be mistaken for anything else. The employment of words is unusual without being odd. A reader who was unacquainted with the usages of poetry, coming unexpectedly upon these phrases would find them surprising, but he would not be tempted to ridicule them. This is not the common way of speech, but the difference is plainly one of heightened power, of elevation in the admirable sense.

English poetry, however, is peculiarly rich in beauties of diction that are achieved by another means. Longinus, at the opening of his essay on the Sublime, says :

the effect of genius is not to persuade the audience but rather to transport them out of themselves. Invariably what inspires wonder casts a spell upon us and is always superior to what is merely convincing and pleasing. For our convictions are usually under our own control, while such passages exercise an irresistible power of mastery and get the upper hand with every member of the audience. Again, inventive skill and the due disposal and marshalling of facts do not show themselves in one or two touches : they gradually emerge from the whole tissue of the composition, while, on the other hand, a well-tuned flash of sublimity scatters everything before it like a bolt of lightning and reveals the full power of the speaker at a single stroke.

Something on this relation between ' the whole tissue of the composition ' and the ' single stroke ' of sublimity has been said in our examination of Wordsworth's leech-gatherer poem. The matter now under consideration is the nature of those ' single strokes ' in poetry, the moments that suddenly excite us to the highest pitch of pleasure and illuminate the whole surrounding tissue of the poem. These often take the form of such obviously exceptional phrases as have just been cited ; but no less often, and in my own view with an even lovelier enchantment, they take the form of words that are of themselves ordinary, familiar, common if you will, and are yet by their placing and context invested with the exceptional quality and the full surprise of authoritative poetic diction. This pleasure seems to be in the gift of poetry alone. The manifestly splendid phrase, made up of words not commonly familiar to speech, is an excellent device of the poets, but it is also within the compass of prose : ' The iniquity of oblivion blindly scattereth her poppy.' But that other magic waits only on the intenser mood of poetry. At least, if examples of it can be found in prose, they are exceedingly rare, whereas in poetry they are abundant. Wordsworth, in his task of ridding poetry of its fustian, explained that his 'purpose was to imitate, and, as far as possible, to adopt the very language of men'. Here was a determination to give common words the life of poetry, but Wordsworth in his doctrine had in mind rather 'the whole tissue of the composition' than the single and enlivening strokes of sublimity. In practice no poet has more frequently achieved his moments of sublimity by the rarer and simpler means than he, but it was towards another end that his theory of poetic diction was directed. His conscious aim as an artist was to keep his poetry throughout spare and homely in form, seeking for it the dignity of that rustic life in which 'men hourly communicate with the best objects from which the best part of language is originally derived'.

> Upon the forest-side in Grasmere Vale
> There dwelt a Shepherd, Michael was his name ;
> An old man, stout of heart, and strong of limb.
> His bodily frame had been from youth to age
> Of an unusual strength : his mind was keen,
> Intense, and frugal, apt for all affairs,
> And in his shepherd's calling he was prompt
> And watchful more than ordinary men.

To emphasize Wordsworth's success in such a passage, we need only contrast it with John Home's curiously celebrated—

> My name is Norval ; on the Grampian hills
> My father feed his flocks ; a frugal swain,
> Whose constant cares were to increase his store,
> And keep his only son, myself, at home,

or, indeed, with less successful passages from Wordsworth himself. It may be said in passing that a certain flatness in poetry, a long way below the level of those lines from *Michael*, does not necessarily, to one reader at least, make it quite unpleasurable. There is a good deal of George Crabbe, for example, that I find to my liking even although the poetic pressure may be said to sink to vanishing point. That, however, is by the way. The four or five hundred lines of *Michael*, taken as a whole, are a notable vindication of Wordsworth's poetic theory. That theory, however, includes the startling assertion that ' there neither is, nor can be, any *essential* difference between the language of prose and metrical composition '. When a great poet says something about his art that seems to be strangely wide of the mark, we confidently expect that he will somehow explain himself, and, sure enough, within a few lines Wordsworth is stipulating that the poet in making ' a selection of the language really spoken by men ', he must make it with ' true taste and feeling ', such as will ' entirely separate the composition from the vulgarity and meanness of ordinary life '. Here then after all is surely the *essential* difference which Wordsworth himself underlines. *Michael* is written in ' the language really spoken by men ', but the selection of that language is made with unerring ' taste and feeling ' by the poet. Nevertheless this general elevation of common speech to the level of genuine poetic diction still does not account for the moments or ' single strokes ' of sublimity that the familiar word can sometimes achieve more magically than the unfamiliar. Two instances have already been quoted in another connexion :

> The grave's *a fine and private place*,

and

> no weakness, no contempt,
> Dispraise or blame, *nothing but well and fair* . . .

to which examples a few others may be added : Henry
King's pledge to his dead wife,

> But hark ! My pulse, like a soft drum
> Beats my approach, tells thee I come ;
> And slow howe'er my marches be,
> *I shall at last sit down by thee.*

The opening line of *The Scholar Gipsy*,

> *Go, for they call you, Shepherd, from the hill ;*

Alice Meynell in *The Shepherdess*,

> She holds her little thoughts in sight,
> Though gay they run and leap.
> She is so circumspect *and right* ;
> She has her soul to keep.

Herrick's,

> When I a verse shall make,
> Know I have prayed thee,
> *For old religion's sake,*
> Saint Ben, to aid me.

Coleridge with,

> 'T is a month before the month of May,
> And *the Spring comes slowly up this way* . . .

and

> whether the eave-drops fall
> Heard only in the trances of the blast,
> Or if the secret ministry of frost
> Shall hang them up in silent icicles,
> *Quietly shining to the quiet moon.*

Tennyson's

> *And the sun went down, and the stars came out far over*
> *the summer sea . . .*

and

> *On one side lay the Ocean, and on one*
> *Lay a great water, and the moon was full.*

The anonymous poet of *Sir Patrick Spens*, superbly, with,

> *The King sits in Dunfermline town*
> Drinking the blood-red wine . . .

and that other of—

> There is a lady sweet and kind,
> Was never face so pleased my mind ;
> *I did but see her passing by,*
> *And yet I love her till I die.*

Ben Jonson to Diana :

> Queen and huntress, chaste and fair,
>   Now the sun is laid to sleep,
> Seated in thy silver chair,
>   State in wonted manner keep :
>   Hesperus entreats thy light,
>   *Goddess excellently bright.*

John Donne's—

> And whilst our souls negotiate there,
>   We like sepulchral statues lay ;
> All day the same our postures were,
>   *And we said nothing, all the day.*

Blake's—

> Till we have built Jerusalem
> *In England's green and pleasant land.*

And, to take one instance from a living poet, W. H. Davies in *The Moon* writes :

> Though there are birds that sing this night
>   With thy white beams across their throats,
> Let my deep silence speak for me
>   More than for them their sweetest notes :
>   Who worships thee till music fails,
>   *Is greater than thy nightingales.*

An anthology of examples might be taken from Shakespeare alone : three will suffice.

> *We are such stuff*
> *As dreams are made on, and our little life*
> *Is rounded with a sleep . . .*

and—

> Speak of me as I am ; nothing extenuate,
> Nor set down aught in malice : *then, must you speak*
> *Of one that lov'd, not wisely, but too well . . .*

and—

> O, that a man might know
> The end of this day's business, ere it come !
> *But it sufficeth, that the day will end,*
> *And then the end is known.*

To take special notice of such particular distinctions is not to overlook the fact that nevertheless in a good poem the whole is greater than even its best parts. But these felicities test us in reading poetry. If as we come to them we do not feel a quickening of the pulse, there is something amiss with our perceptive faculty. There is no good poem that does not contain some sudden heightening of the creative pitch, some ' simple

4

strokes of sublimity', whether they come through
words that are 'unfamiliar' or words that are 'com-
mon'.   Consequently, if in reading poetry we do not
at intervals experience an excitement that as Longinus
says transports us out of ourselves and casts a spell
upon us, either the poetry is insufficient or we are out
of tune.   If the poetry that we are reading is among
that which has been widely accepted by critical judge-
ment, we may take it that it is good poetry, and failing
the inspiration of 'wonder' we may also take it that
the failure is not in the poet but in ourselves.   The
reader, when he sets out on his voyage, may be sure of
this : the poet, worthy of the name, has surrendered
nothing to expediency.   For, to use Longinus again,
' it is not right to display an unseemly triviality before
an audience of all the ages '.

V

AS IT WAS IN THE BEGINNING

HAVING discussed the nature of poetry, the quality of the pleasure for which we look in it, and the relationship between the poet and his reader, we may proceed to the broader question of how best we may visualize poetry (that is, English poetry) as a whole. To read one great lyric with exact appreciation of its beauty is in a way to experience the highest delight that poetry can afford, just as a man who knew *Macbeth* and *Twelfth Night* thoroughly, but nothing else of Shakespeare, might nevertheless in essential respects be said to have the full measure of the dramatist's invention. Abstract principles, however, seldom carry us very far in practice, and the plain fact is that if we are deeply moved by one poem we shall want to know more, and if our imaginative curiosity is genuinely stirred by one adventure in English poetry we shall in all probability find ourselves gradually exploring the whole of it.

In other words, we shall pass from a haphazard to a more or less organized method of reading, and find that the organization is a pleasure in itself. There are two ways of doing this. Poetry can be considered in its chronological sequence, with a genealogy as significant as that of the race. The satisfaction derived from a lyric by Ralph Hodgson may be the same in spiritual essence as that derived from a lyric by Chaucer, but it is a matter of absorbing interest to follow the long road that poetry has travelled between the two. Secondly, there is a natural inclination to relate a particular kind of poetry in one age to its complement in another. To read *The Earthly Paradise* or *Reynard the Fox* is instinctively to be reminded of *The Canterbury Tales*.

The organic growth or continuity of English poetry leads us into a wide field of speculation. One of the oldest and most controversial problems of literary criticism is that of deciding how much or how little the artist should reflect or interpret his own age in his work. Not for an age but for all time was Ben Jonson's praise of Shakespeare, while Bernard Shaw, who more than any other modern writer is Jonson's intellectual inheritor, insists that if an artist is not pre-eminently for his own age he is for no age at all. Jonson himself, who of all our great dramatic poets is least honoured by popular favour in measure with his merit, has suffered much by his failure to observe the standard that he so much admired in Shakespeare. His plays have a superb dramatic vitality that still makes them exciting when they are performed in the theatre, but they are burdened with a weight of contemporary allusion, social and scholastic, that impedes their free progress on the stage for us to-day. The idiom of Shakespeare's dramatic action is no less coloured by Elizabethan life than Jonson's, but whereas with Shakespeare this is an influence on his manner of speaking, with Jonson it is largely the origin and substance of his material. The Elizabethan theatre produced nothing finer of its kind than the robust splendour of *The Alchemist*, and yet the grand humour and rhetorical energy of the piece miss some of their effect for us because they are occasioned by a subject that does not intimately concern us.   Jonson, it is true, in vigorous ridicule of the quackery that infested the science of his time, says much that has permanent application, but the subject and its treatment as a whole are insufficiently redeemed from fugitive social circumstance to give them—as a whole—durable significance.   Even Shakespeare could not have excelled the invention and the vehemence of *The Alchemist*, but it is impossible to think of Shakespeare choosing the subject of *The Alchemist* for a play.

A similar contrast may be made between Ibsen's *Ghosts* and Shaw's *Widowers' Houses*.   It may now be accepted as an established fact that in the renascence of the English theatre during the past fifty years Mr. Shaw will remain the most commanding figure ; that is to say, we have, with the possible exceptions of Sheridan and Goldsmith, to go back to Congreve to find his match.   It is, indeed, one of the less agreeable aspects of the popular attitude towards the theatre to-day that, after his long and proved achievement, any new work of his on the stage should not draw every intelligent playgoer in the country as a matter of course.   His later plays may have defects that are easy money to any small critic, but what living dramatist, native or foreign, could write anything to rival *On the Rocks* and *Too True to be Good* on their own ground ?   It is then, I hope, with due recognition of his remarkable powers that for the present purpose emphasis is laid on certain perishable elements in his work.   Some of his plays are less disturbed by these than others, but *Widowers' Houses* is as good an example as any of their presence. Even though the invective of Jonson's verse rises above the banter of Shaw's prose, the dialectic of this piece is as spirited as that of *The Alchemist* ; that is to say, it stands up to the highest standard. And yet, if the play is compared with *Ghosts* it is seen to have ' dated ' in a manner that is not wholly accounted for by Ibsen's choice of a more universal theme. For if either *An Enemy of the People* or *Pillars of Society* be substituted for *Ghosts,* much the same consideration holds good. The explanation is that whereas in the Ibsen plays the dramatist's passionate social conscience is steadily sub-dued to a higher creative instinct, in *Widowers' Houses* an equally passionate social conscience frequently takes control and becomes the end rather than the occasion of the creative function. The result may be seen more clearly if we reflect upon the difference of effect made upon us by the one and the other. We retain an acute interest in Ibsen's people irrespective of what they are doing, while we remember the people of *Widowers' Houses* chiefly for their social designs and misdemeanours, and but dimly for what they are. It follows that when those social designs have ceased to have a topical import we have difficulty in remembering the people at all, and it is a fact that in our recollection Dr. Stockmann is much more clearly a three-dimensional person than Sartorius.

The truth is that although as a creative propagandist Shaw is Ibsen's or any one else's equal, he is less than Ibsen as a poet. Inspired tractarians are rare enough in any case, and when we find one who is a first-rate dramatic craftsman and a bonny wit into the bargain, we may thank heaven for the chance of more than a lifetime. But poetry still stands where it did, and it is not where Mr. Shaw stands. In his quick-footed resilient prose he achieves an undeniable beauty of his own, but for my own part I admire him least when he most deliberately ' feigns poetical ', as in the first and last parts of *Back to Methuselah* and the angelic apparatus of *Saint Joan*. I have always supposed, mistakenly it may be, that Marjoribanks in *Candida* was intended, subconsciously perhaps, to be in some measure a modern incarnation of Shelley, and when seeing that almost perfect comedy have always wanted to stand up and tell the author that in this his copy is egregiously unlike the original. Having thus twisted a great man's work to my purpose, I take my present leave of him, reminding myself that I once dedicated a play to him ' with homage to the master dramatist of his age, and with the gratitude that is his due from every younger writer for the English Theatre ', and that I would gladly dedicate another one to-morrow in the same terms.

Our reasoning leads to the position that poetry establishes itself by qualities that are wholly independent of its capacity for reflecting a particular age. The most notable example in the language of what we mean is *Paradise Lost*, the general argument of which is largely based on an obsolete theology in which no one to-day can take anything but a pedantic interest at most. And yet what in the matter of our intellectual interest might be accounted a defect in the poem does not in the least detract from its poetic achievement nor from our pleasure in it. We do not believe in the literal fable of *Paradise Lost* ; we may even go beyond that and say that Milton certainly did not believe in it himself. Further, the often made claim that in spite of his lip service to God Milton's real sympathy was with the Satan of his invention, is not without plausibility. Which means that he also had no great enthusiasm for his own theological doctrine. It may be retorted that if these things were so, if Milton had little or no real faith either in his fable

or his doctrine, he was culpable of an attempted decep-
tion that must be inimical to the essential truth that is
the very spirit of poetry.   But it is precisely this essential
truth that was in no way violated by the poet's employ-
ment of a conventional mould into which to pour the
molten ore of his creative genius.   What was necessary
to Milton was not that he should believe literally in
the fable and theology of his poem, but that these should
have a grandeur of scope in which he could exercise
freely the sublimity of his poetic conception.

For this conception, we note, was something larger
than the fable and theology of *Paradise Lost*, something
in which these were not inherent.   Many years before
the composition of that poem was begun, he tells us
himself, he had dedicated his life to the hope of leaving
' something so written to aftertimes, as they should not
willingly let it die ', of doing for his country ' what the
greatest and choicest wits of Athens, Rome, or modern
Italy, and those Hebrews of old ' had done for theirs.
The truth and life of poetry on a grand scale were already
working strongly within him, and his practical problem
was to make deliberate choice of a suitable subject or
occasion to release them.   He tells us of the many
themes that engaged his attention, as some ' King or
Knight, before the conquest, in whom to lay the pattern
of a Christian hero ', or the Song of Solomon, or the
Apocalypse of Saint John, these and others finally to be
rejected in favour of the story of the fall and redemption
of man.   In other words, the choice was an arbitrary
one, but, having been made, its service was to be the
embodiment of the poetic life that had been generating
for years, governed always by the resolution to describe
' whatsoever in religion is holy and sublime, in virtue
amiable or grave, whatsoever hath passion or admira-

tion in all the changes of that which is called fortune from without, or the wily subtleties and refluxes of man's thoughts from within '. Any fable and doctrinal formality that would enable him to do this with the full power of his poetry were sufficient. His duty was, as Aristotle bade, to ' show invention and make a skilful use of the tradition '.

How splendid were the invention and skill that he employed, *Paradise Lost* remains to show. The literal truth of Milton's fable and doctrine become matters of no consequence when illuminated by the transcendental truth of his poetry. Cardinal Newman, discussing Aristotle's *Poetics*, observed that the Greek philosopher's theory of tragic plot was far less exactly satisfied by the Greek poets than has commonly been supposed. Aristotle, he says, ' rather tells us what tragedy should be, than what Greek tragedy really was . . . That the charm of Greek tragedy does not ordinarily arise from scientific correctness of plot, is certain as a matter of fact.' Newman proceeds to substantiate the statement by convincing instances drawn from Aeschylus, Sophocles, and Euripides. Then :

Thus the Greek drama, as a fact, was modelled on no scientific principle. It was a pure recreation of the imagination, revelling without object or meaning beyond its own exhibition . . . Why interrupt so divine a display of poetical genius by inquiries degrading it to the level of everyday events . . . ? The very spirit of beauty breathes through ever part of the composition.

It is so in *Paradise Lost*.

To examine the chronological procession of poetry, then, in the hope of discovering what, sometimes rightly and sometimes wrongly, is regarded as social or intellectual progress, is to look for what we shall not find. When Shelley said that poets were the unacknowledged legislators of the world, he announced the profound truth that the undercurrents of poetry exercise an influence upon human affairs that cannot be measured. But, beyond this, there are many things that poetry directly cannot and has no desire to do. Poetry has no part in the demagogic or minority politics, in the sensations of to-day that are the oblivion of to-morrow, the sad little fallacies of men who are persuaded that the world was created on the day of their own nativity. Such topics may promote cultivated verse that is more self-confident if less effective than the more usual forms of journalism, but they do not attract the attention of the most lovely as she is the most powerful of the Muses. A fugitive necessity is a necessity none the less, but it is idle to confuse it with the durable conditions in which not only we but also the generations live. Fashion is by no means contemptible : it is an amusing circumstance of life. But poetry does not abide by fashion. Seventeen hundred years ago Longinus, whose very name is guesswork, wrote : ' all these improprieties in literature are weeds sprung from the same seed, namely that passion for novel ideas, which is the prevalent craze of the present day '.

> Still crowned with bay each ancient altar stands
> Above the reach of sacrilegious hands.

And so let us approach the altars on, I trust, a ground sufficiently cleared.

VI

POETRY AND NARRATIVE (1)

THE popularity of any specific literary work is notoriously an uncertain criterion of merit, but the permanence of a literary form in popular favour cannot but indicate a basic fitness. Of all literary forms, or figures, the story has, first and last, most taken the fancy of men.

Criticism has sometimes sought, unsuccessfully I think, to identify the ejaculations of primal life in its ooze with the first expressions of lyric poetry. Within more measurable horizons of experience, the lyric appears to have waited on a later development of society than narrative. In any case, we may say with certainty that effective appeal from the poet to an audience has always been made earlier and more easily by a tale about something than by a recital of his own emotions about something. This is not to place narrative either below or above lyric in art. There is no aesthetic theory by which lyric could be shown to be less necessary to the full consummation of poetic achievement as a whole than narrative, but there is ample reason for concluding that in the long progress of literature it is the story that has been the form most generally desired. That narrative has commonly, and particularly in later times, forsaken verse for prose makes no matter.

It is therefore not surprising to find that the first work in English poetry, or English literature, to reach undoubted greatness and also to establish a lasting hold on popular favour, was a narrative poem, or rather a series of narrative poems so conceived and arranged as to make an organic whole. To say that England before *The Canterbury Tales* had no poetry would be a patent exaggeration, but it had none that was not written in what for us to-day is virtually a foreign tongue, and none that for the past three hundred years has had any claim to popular significance, or any appreciable influence on the practice of the poets. Chaucer changed all that at a stroke. To know nothing before Chaucer is to miss nothing essential to a broad knowledge of English poetry, but not to know Chaucer is to lack knowledge of a yet living source from which English poetry has never ceased to draw. No poet in modern times owes anything considerable to Chaucer's predecessors, but no narrative verse in England since his time, from the heroics of Samuel Daniel and Michael Drayton to William Morris's *Earthly Paradise* and Mr. Masefield's *Reynard the Fox*, is without clear obligation to Chaucer himself.

Nor does Chaucer's achievement distinguish him only from his predecessors. William Langland, John Gower, and the unknown poet of *Pearl* were his contemporaries, and yet their work lies hardly less remotely in the background of our consciousness than the almost inaccessible cadences of *Beowulf*. *Piers Plowman* is a work of impressive merit, and we all know the bits about the Malvern Hills and the fair field full of folk. Also, as Saintsbury points out, the multiplicity of its manuscripts indicates that it was widely popular in its time. But it belongs to a world that has gone out of our familiar

ken, and the reader would be rare to find to-day who
has read the whole of it for delight. *Pearl* is yet further
from our necessities. Its tender allegory, even when
elucidated by Sir Israel Gollancz's devoted if somewhat
unlyrical rendering into modern English, survives in
no more than a faint charm from a manner that is obso-
lete. As for Gower's gigantic *Confessio Amantis*, a poem
four times the length of *Paradise Lost*, it is of a texture
altogether too thin to support its inordinate length. It
has occasional graces that may well have charmed
Richard the Second, the King for whom it was written,
and may, if we persevere in our search for them, charm
us still. But the whole is insupportably diffuse, and
lacks any governing vitality that could induce a modern
reader to explore its wilderness of fable unless he were
compelled to. We rightly honour these poets, who
testified honourably in their time, but we no longer
turn to them naturally for the pleasures of poetry. *The
Canterbury Tales*, *Piers Plowman*, *Confessio Amantis* and
Pearl all belong to the same generation, the last of the
fourteenth century, but while all three poets drew
largely upon the same literary elements from the past,
Chaucer alone kindled from them beacons for the
future.

This, perhaps, is but another way of saying that no
poet in England down to his time, not even one of so
generous a scope as Langland, had anything approach-
ing Chaucer's wealth of creative energy, of his genius
in short. Langland and Gower were figures of large
importance in their time, they have worthy if obscure
places in English poetry, and for some years after their
work was a source of literary activity, but little or
nothing of any consequence in our verse is due to their
direct influence. Even the poets who were their im-

mediate or near successors knew in honouring them
that Chaucer was master of them all. Thomas Hoc-
cleve, writing at the date of Chaucer's death, exclaimed—

> She might have tarried her vengeance awhile,
> Till that some man had equal to thee be !
> Nay ! let be that ! She knew well that this Isle
> May never man forth bringè like to thee . . .

and near a century later William Dunbar took up the
note with—

> He has done piteously devour
> The noble Chaucer, of Makaris flower !
> The Monk of Bury, and Gower, all three !
> *Timor Mortis conturbat me !*

Chaucer in his age was veritably ' of makers flower ',
and, setting the claims of scholarship aside, which are
not here our concern, if we know him and no one else
in English poetry until the publication of *Tottel's Misce-
lany* in 1557 we shall do well enough. It is true that
John Skelton, laureate to Henry the Eighth, expressed
a lively wit with an insufficient art that to-day engages
curiosity rather than admiration, though it has been
much and, I think, extravagantly praised by one or two
recent critics, while a sufficient familiarity with the dialect
may discover in the Scottish poets, James the First,
Dunbar, and Robert Henryson, a quality not to be
matched by any named writer south of the border
during the barren years of the fifteenth century. I say
named, since if, as is most likely, the anonymous group
of poetry known generically as The Ballads belong
chiefly to the fifteenth century, they obviously have to
be excluded from the generalization. They will be
considered later.

Chaucer's language, on which much learning has been employed, presents no serious difficulty to the un-learned reader. Hoccleve five hundred years ago saluted him as 'The first Finder of our fair language', and in all essentials he is still so near to modern usage that after a few pages we can accommodate eye and ear to his verse easily enough without special knowledge. If we choose to vex ourselves with a glossary we shall need it but seldom, and if at first an occasional line sags or clogs, these syllabic difficulties are soon forgotten. Such difference as there is between his language and our own rapidly becomes a pleasure rather than an obstacle, as though we were enjoying the satisfaction of knowing a new tongue without the labour of learning it.

If Chaucer had written nothing but *Troilus and Criseyde* and *The Legend of Good Women*, he would still have excelled his predecessors, but in *The Canterbury Tales* he left the rest of his achievement far behind and became the first great English poet, with no one to share his eminence until the coming of the Elizabethans two hundred years later. With these tales the living delight of English poetry begins, to be suspended as unaccount-ably as it had appeared, and then to rewake at the end of the sixteenth century with a splendour that it was never wholly to lose.

Two things are immediately remarkable about Chaucer's principal poem. The first is that although it came into being unannounced by previous effort, there is nothing tentative or experimental in its char-acter. It has all the mature assurance of those later masters, Shakespeare chief among them, whose achieve-ment it was to give crowning expression to the genius of an age, transcending their time as clearly as they were part of it. I may be told that this view is the result merely of an ignorance of Chaucer's sources, and that an adequate knowledge of his artistic ancestry and environment would show that he too in his mastery was a consummation no less than these others. I do not think that the objection can hold. It needs no great erudition to see what are quite simple matters of fact, which have, indeed, sometimes been obscured by pedantry. Chaucer borrowed some of his narrative conventions and some of his fables from earlier writers. This was neither to his credit nor otherwise. Shakespeare did the same thing, so conspicuously as to furnish generations of critics with ingenious occasions. But it remains a question of little more than academic interest. Shakespeare's practice in the matter was merely an accident of his working career, and should not for a moment be confused with his supremely representative character. That depended on far weightier considerations than the chance that he borrowed material from other men and bettered the instruction. He acquired it because he was able to enrich and perfect in his own words the throbbing vitality of an age immensely rich in life, in thought, in action and in literature—particularly, it is to be noted, already in literature. He did better than any one else what many men in the preceding decade or two and in his own time had been and were doing notably well. He was recognized by his contemporaries as a master, but, even so, as a master among many masters. The surge and passion of his poetry was the apotheosis not only of a great society but also of a great literature already worthily commemorating that society. He overtopped a company of giants.

Chaucer's was a very different case. He, like Shakespeare, made good use of borrowed material, but there the similarity ends. The term that most fitly embraces all the qualities of Shakespeare's work is vitality, and we know the source from which his vitality was derived, or by which, perhaps, we should say, apart from its own nature it was chiefly fortified. It is not claiming equality for Chaucer with Shakespeare as a poet to say that in this cardinal virtue of vitality he was hardly less than the greater man. But from what source outside its own nature was Chaucer's vitality notably fortified? He grew up in a position of some small importance at the court of Edward the Third, a robust if not entirely civilizing experience, but *The Canterbury Tales* was written when England under Richard the Second had slender reason to be either in high spirits or proud of itself. Certainly the vitality of the poem, its clean-cut, crisp enjoyment of character for its own sake, its acute good-humour, its nervous intensity of action, and its lyric freshness rich as April buds, were no reflection of a national life rejoicing in its own abundance. Even less, if less were possible, was this excellence the culminating performance of a prevalent national literature. Nowhere in Chaucer's England could be found any example approaching his achievement in kind, let alone degree. On an Italian mission he is said to have met Boccaccio, and something in the spirit of his work derived from this and other continental contacts. But when all such allowance is made, the native quality of *The Canterbury Tales* is saturated with the English temper. And it is presented with an art that in any circumstances would have been masterly, but in isolation was a miracle.

The second immediately notable thing about the poem is the necessity of verse to Chaucer as a poet. This is by no means the commonplace that at first sight it may appear. We are not now looking at English

5

poetry in the light of five hundred years' experience, but on its inception. Chaucer is the first English writer to whom a place in the front rank of the world's literature can be assigned. In using verse as his medium he made a choice that has been significant to the whole course of the English genius. To say that England has no great writers of prose would manifestly be absurd, but it can reasonably be claimed that with none but its poets in verse English literature would still be a major glory of civilization while without them it would not. This view would seem to imply that verse has some quite independent virtue of its own, and this in fact is so. Just as all life itself is a mystery, so all expressions of life are mysterious also, defying complete analysis. For myself I gladly confess to nothing but impatience with the school of aesthetic criticism that seeks to reduce the nature of art to terms of diagrams on a blackboard, and I once had the pleasure of simulating faintness in order to get out of a crowded room during such a demonstration. But behind these frivolities there is an intelligible desire to get beyond barriers that baffle us. In the theory of literature there is, I think, nothing quite so evasive as this problem of the nature of verse. One thing about it, however, at any rate is clear. Verse *has* a life of its own which cannot be explained by reference simply to its literal meaning or its diction or its cadence. In my book on Shakespeare I claimed that his verse was in itself a sovran element of his drama, and Lytton Strachey in his essay on Pope pointed out that beyond his intellect and wit his command of the heroic couplet was the secret of his genius. Verse, in other words, is not merely a way of saying something, it is itself something said. Verse, and I mean good verse, since in our reckoning bad verse is a contradiction in terms, has its own integrity in literature as surely as light upon a landscape has in nature.

To us, with the record of the ages for our precept, this is clear enough, but it was no less than a divine instinct that led the originators, Homer, and some Icelandic bard, and Chaucer to the truth. Chaucer's material was, as it happens, of a kind that might have seemed to be readily accessible to prose. In two of his *Tales*, that of Melibeus and the Parson's, he actually used prose, with miserable results. They could be removed from the Canterbury canon with no loss whatever. There they are, however, and the candid reader will skip them.

Having franked my own pass to travel as I will, I shall here digress or outrun myself by some centuries. Chaucer at the dawn of our literature put verse in command. Two hundred years later Shakespeare and his fellows gave magnificent emphasis to the authority. The Miltonic age speaks for itself in its name. Then Dryden, Pope, Wordsworth, Coleridge, Byron, Shelley, Keats, Tennyson, with a dozen to match them, maintain the supremacy. Walter Scott forsook verse for prose only as a readier means of making a living under the challenge of Byron's popularity : George Meredith set more store by his poems than by his library of novels : and Thomas Hardy, probably the greatest novelist in the language, laboured magnificently in prose, but saw Pisgah-land in verse.

And then we come to our own time with its astounding avalanche of prose fiction, so much of it admirable and exquisite among the spate of rubbish and froth. Where, it may be asked—it often is asked—do the poets stand now ? And the answer is that, with Dan Chaucer as the jargon of his age called him, they stand very hopefully indeed. Walter de la Mare may not, certainly he does not, earn such royalties as Hugh Walpole, whose work I enthusiastically admire, but somewhere about A.D. 2500 I'll put my sixpence on *The Listeners* against the very fine Herries saga. That other noble saga, too, of the Forsytes, can never fail in interest for any reader who is curious as to the social significance of our time, but in that same far-distant date one enchanted scholar will explore it for ten common men who will say to themselves a verse by W. B. Yeats as they walk along a reconstructed Strand. And what chance of survival have the pastoral melodies of so fine a work as *The Rainbow* against W. H. Davies's song to the moon—

> Though there are birds that sing this night
> 　With thy white beams across their throats,
> Let my deep silence speak for me
> 　More than for them their sweetest notes :
> Who worships thee till music fails
> Is greater than thy nightingales . . .

or, indeed, half a dozen of D. H. Lawrence's own poems ?

Like all great story-tellers, Chaucer is leisurely in his method. If under the influence of the cinema and the quick-fire fiction of the magazines we have cultivated impatient minds and want our amusement to be snappy, we shall not turn to Chaucer. But then neither shall we turn to Cervantes or Fielding or Dumas or Walter Scott or Hardy. With all these men the plot or basic action of a tale was of less importance than the manner of telling it. Or, more exactly, it was in the manner of telling it that the plot took on its real life and substance. To reduce the plot of any narrative masterpiece to a *précis* is to substitute for the original something that may have some logical but certainly has no artistic resemblance to it.   That is why the attempts of dramatic critics to summarize the story of a play in their notices are usually so futile, or more often positively misleading. The poet, says Philip Sidney, ' entices ' us to his company : ' with a tale, forsooth, he cometh unto you, with a tale which holdeth children from play, and old men from the chimney corner '.   We are to be beguiled into listening, not bawled.   So it is with Chaucer. When April stirs the earth to renewal, he tells us at the outset, ' then longen folk to goon on pilgrimages '. We set out on a pilgrimage with him, and it is a long one.   With no haste to come to the end of the journey we are to keep open eyes for everything on the highway and at the wayside.   There is purpose always in our travelling, but there must be no anxiety, no refusal of reflection as we go.

The Canterbury Tales as a single poem was never completed in accordance with Chaucer's design, nor as they stand is there evidence of any formal arrangement. The machinery of the Canterbury pilgrims telling their tales in turn with the Host as chorus or master of the ceremonies, and prologues in which Chaucer may be said to be speaking for himself, gives a semblance of organic unity to the work, but externally the general effect remains one of a series of tales, having no obvious connexion with each other, and loosely assembled by a pleasant device of no great significance.   And yet to read one of the stories by itself is by no means to receive the same impression as is made by a reading of the whole, even in its truncated form.   It is only then that we see how thoroughly the poet has transmuted his mixed material, taken from the romance of chivalry,

classical and biblical legend, and the common stock of
continental and native fable, into a perfectly acclimatized
English idiom of thought, speech, and character. In
the wide variety of his subject-matter Chaucer shows a
pretty considerable cosmopolitan learning, but he wears
it always lightly, without the least parade, and he hardly
ever moralizes his knowledge. He is a cultivated
Englishman, schooled in many classes of society, enjoy-
ing the spectacle of his countrymen going about their
daily business, and recording it shrewdly, humorously,
on occasion tenderly, but seldom with either transport
or indignation. It is a sunny, fragrant world in which
he moves, a world of shining April and May—autumnal
imagery is almost unknown in his poetry—not without
stratagems and mischief, but not much given to high
passions, a quiet world always.

Chaucer's work as an originator imposed on him the
heavy responsibilities of leadership, but it also gave him
certain privileges. It was against all probability that
he accomplished what he did at all in the circumstances,
but, being endowed with the genius to do it, the cir-
cumstances in some ways were to his advantage. He
wrote English as it had never been written before, and
in laying the linguistic foundations of all our later
literature he displayed an energy so great as to be almost
beyond our comprehension. If we think of all the
English poetry since his time, and then realize that
when he sat down to write *The Canterbury Tales* none
of it was in existence, we can form some dim con-
ception of the magnitude of his task and the triumph
of its achievement. On the other hand, once his as-
tonishing power had asserted itself, he found himself
employing an instrument of unimpaired freshness.
Words had not been staled by repetition, and the

simplest phrase was absolved from the commonplace. Throughout his verse we find an elemental, one might almost say an elementary diction. To say that a bird sang, that a woman was fair, that the poet was full glad, that the grass was green and the flowers sweet, was enough. His observation was alert, his emotion sensitive, but they needed no more than this extreme simplification of record. The remarkable thing is that as we read him five hundred years later these phrases still fall on the ear with the same delighted discovery that he experienced when he wrote them. A notable passage in Thomas Campbell's *Essay on English Poetry* says :

Every rock, every leaf, every diversity of hue in nature's variety ! Assuredly this botanizing perspicacity might be essential to a Dutch flower-painter ; but Sophocles displays no such skill, and yet he is a genuine, a great, and affecting poet. Even in describing the desert island of Philoctetes, there is no minute observation of nature's hues in secret places. Throughout the Greek tragedians there is nothing to show them more attentive observers of inanimate objects than other men.

That is well said, though the last sentence seems to carry the argument a little too far. Chaucer is a case in point no less than the Greek tragedians. The ' botanizing ', which Tennyson for example in a more sophisticated age of poetry often put to justly admired use, was wholly foreign to Chaucer's aim and necessity. But the spareness of the earlier poet's statement is no evidence that he was a less ' attentive observer ' than the later. Tennyson's minute elaboration of an image is often lovely, but certainly no lovelier than Chaucer's abridgement.

This passeth yeer by yeer, and day by day,
Til it fil ones, in a morwe of May,
That Emelye, that fairer was to sene
Than is the lilie upon his stalke grene,
And fressher than the May with floures newe—
For with the rose colour stroof hir hewe,
I noot which was the fairer of hem two—
Er it were day, as was hir wone to do,
She was arisen, and al redy dight ;
For May wol have no slogardye a-night.
The sesoun priketh every gentil herte,
And maketh him out of his sleep to sterte,
And seith, ' Arys, and do thyn observaunce.'
This maked Emelye have remembraunce
To doon honour to May, and for to ryse.
Y-clothed was she fresh, for to devyse ;
Hir yelow heer was broyded in a tresse,
Bihinde hir bak, a yerde long, I gesse.
And in the gardin, at the sonne up-riste,
She walketh up and doun, and as hir liste
She gadereth floures, party whyte and rede,
To make a sotil gerland for hir hede,
And as an aungel hevenly she song.

The lily on its green stalk, the yellow hair, the white
and red flowers, so seeming-artless in their statement,
have still the unfaded brilliance of primary colours in
an illuminated missal. And surely traveller never found
nature more magically enchanting that Sir Thopas riding
through ' a fair forest ' :

Ther springen herbes grete and smale,
The lycorys and cetewale,
And many a clowe-gilofre ;
And notemuge to putte in ale,
Whether it be moyste or stale,
Or for to leye in cofre.

The briddes singe, it is no nay,
The sparhauk and the papejay,
   That joye it was to here ;
The thrustelcok made eek his lay,
The wodedowve upon the spray
   She sang ful loude and clere.

If the movement of Chaucer's narrative is usually
deliberate, he could contrive breathless moments of
dramatic suspense when he chose to. The management
of the messenger and the letters in the Man of Law's
Tale of Custance shows a command of action that would
have graced the Elizabethan stage itself, and the three
drunken ' ryotoures ' in The Pardoner's Tale setting out
to slay Death are figures that might keep company with
Macbeth's witches or the eldritch queans of Tam
o' Shanter. In principle, however, the story in Chaucer
is a means to an end rather than an end in itself. Philip
Sidney, when he speaks about the poet holding children
from play and old men from the chimney corner with
a tale, very significantly proceeds, ' and, pretending no
more, doth intend the winning of the mind from
wickedness to virtue ; even as a child is often brought
to take most wholesome things, by hiding them in such
others as have a pleasant taste '. Had he wished to
cite an example, no one could have served his purpose
more fitly than Chaucer. Clearly he is using the words
wickedness and virtue in a figurative sense, as meaning
spiritual vigilance and spiritual sloth. Chaucer's tales
always have a pleasant taste, and he is too skilful a crafts-
man ever to let it be seen that he is using them for any
but their own purposes. Their development, though
leisurely, is broken only by digressions so discreet as
never to tax the patience of a reader intent on the
fortunes of the protagonists. Nevertheless, concealed

within the poet's art is a steadfast purpose if not precisely
to win us to virtue at least to delight himself in virtue,
the virtue of reflection on human character, and moral
issues, and natural beauty, and the processes of science
and art, and love, and political philosophy, and the ways
of God to man—in short, on everything that life presented
to the acutest and most poetical mind of the fourteenth
century in England. The firmly designed framework
of his stories encloses a world of free speculation on these
themes, and it is in such speculation that the essential
quality of his work is to be found.

Wide as was the range of his speculation—and the
catalogue just given of its topics could readily be en-
larged—the aspects of life that outran all others in their
interest for him were natural beauty and human character.
The freshness of green fields and singing birds and
bright rivers and sweet-smelling flowers and sunlight is
a continual undertone or obligato to his work. Char-
acteristic passages have already been given. The open-
ing lines of *The Canterbury Tales* give a clear lead to
the temper of the whole :

> Whan that Aprille with his shoures sote
> The droghte of Marche hath perced to the rote,
> And bathed every veyne in swich licour,
> Of which vertu engendred is the flour ;
> Whan Zephirus eek with his swete breeth
> Inspired hath in every holt and heeth
> The tendre croppes, and the yonge sonne
> Hath in the Ram his halfe cours y-ronne,
> And smale fowle maken melodye,
> That slepen al the night with open yë,
> (So priketh hem nature in hir corages) :
> Than longen folk to goon on pilgrimages . . .

As Arcite goes out for his May garland—

The bisy larke, messager of day,
Saluëth in hir song the morwe gray ;
And fyry Phebus ryseth up so brighte,
That al the orient laugheth of the lighte,
And with his stremes dryeth in the greves
The silver dropes, hanging on the leves.
And Arcite, that is in the court royal
With Theseus, his squyer principal,
Is risen, and loketh on the myrie day.
And, for to doon his observaunce to May,
Remembring on the poynt of his desyr,
He on a courser, sterting as the fyr,
Is riden in-to the feeldes, him to pleye,
Out of the court, were it a myle or tweye ;
And to the grove, of which that I yow tolde,
By aventure, his wey he gan to holde,
To maken him a gerland of the greves,
Were it of wodebinde or hawethorn-leves,
And loude he song ageyn the sonne shene :
' May, with alle thy floures and thy grene,
Wel-come be thou, faire fresshe May,
I hope that I som grene gete may.'

Of the carpenter's amorous young wife in The Miller's
Tale we are told—

> hir song, it was as loude and yerne
> As any swalwe sitting on a berne,

and

> Hir mouth was swete as bragot or the meeth,
> Or hord of apples leyd in hay or heeth—

a harvest touch in this last that is rare in Chaucer.
The 'prentice in the fragment of The Cook's Tale—
' Gaillard was he as goldfinch in the shawe ', and the
Shipman's Merchant claimed in kinship by the monk

made no disclaimer, ' but was as glad ther-of as fowel of day '. The Host, chiding the monk for telling them of melancholy fortunes, exclaims :

> Your tale anoyeth all this companye ;
> Swich talking is nat worth a boterflye.

Dorigen's women in The Franklin's Tale, hoping to distract her mind from the long vigil for her husband's ship, tempt her :

> So on a day, right in the morwe-tyde,
> Un-to a gardin that was ther bisyde,
> In which that they had maad hir ordinaunce
> Of vitaille and of other purveyaunce,
> They goon and pleye hem al the longe day.
> And this was on the sixte morwe of May,
> Which May had peynted with his softe shoures
> This gardin ful of leves and of floures ;
> And craft of mannes hand so curiously
> Arrayed hadde this gardin, trewely,
> That never was ther gardin of swich prys,
> But-if it were the verray paradys.
> Th' odour of floures and the fresshe sighte
> Wolde han maad any herte for to lighte
> That ever was born, but-if to gret siknesse,
> Or to gret sorwe helde it in distresse ;
> So ful it was of beautee with plesaunce.

In short, the gaiety of nature conditioned the mood of Chaucer's poetry throughout his career, as surely at the end of *The Canterbury Tales* as in his early rendering of *The Romaunt of The Rose* :

> And ofte tyme, him to solace,
> Sir Mirthe cometh into this place,
> And eek with him cometh his meynee,
> That liven in lust and jolitee.

> And now is Mirthe therin, to here
> The briddes, how they singen clere,
> The mavis and the nightingale,
> And other joly briddes smale. . . .

Chaucer was the first English writer to take any important interest in character, using the term not in the broader Greek sense of fate but in the narrower though more particularized sense of personality. Indeed, it may be questioned whether anywhere in literature before his time there is to be found a gift to match his for this kind of observation, and whether any one since has been his better. His Knight may be a stock figure taken over from the age of chivalry, but how deft and how completely he is presented in six lines :

> And evermore he hadde a sovereyn prys.
> And though that he were worthy, he was wys,
> And of his port as meke as is a mayde.
> He never yet no vileinye ne sayde
> In al his lyf, un-to no maner wight.
> He was a verray parfit gentil knight.

Sometimes illumination comes of the slightest word, as this of the Monk :

> He was nat pale as a for-pyned goost.
> A fat swan loved he best of any roost—

or this of the Friar :

> His eyen twinkled in his heed aright,
> As doon the sterres in the frosty night—

or again this of the Man of Law :

> No-when so bisy a man as he ther nas,
> And yet he semed bisier than he was ;

and this of the Priest :

> A bettre preest, I trowe that nowher noon is.
> He wayted after no pompe and reverence,
> Ne maked him a spyced conscience,
> But Cristes lore, and his apostles twelve,
> He taughte, and first he folwed it himselve.

The Franklin, whose beard was as white as a daisy, was shown as an epicure, so he loved a sop-in-wine, and

> Ful many a fat partrich hadde he in mewe,
> And many a breem and many a luce in stewe.

An infirmity apart, we are told nothing of the Cook but his culinary skill, appetizingly enough :

> A Cook they hadde with hem for the nones,
> To boille the chiknes with the marybones,
> And poudre-marchant tart, and galingale.
> Wel coude he knowe a draughte of London ale.
> He coude roste, and sethe, and broille, and frye,
> Maken mortreux, and wel bake a pye.
> But greet harm was it, as it thoughte me,
> That on his shine a mormal hadde he ;
> For blankmanger, that made he with the beste.

But of the Clerk of Oxenford we learn as much in twenty-four lines as many an expert novelist would tell us in as many pages :

> A Clerk ther was of Oxenford also,
> That un-to logik hadde longe y-go.
> As lene was his hors as is a rake,
> And he nas nat right fat, I undertake ;
> But loked holwe, and ther-to soberly.
> Ful thredbar was his overest courtepy ;
> For he had geten him yet no benefyce,
> Ne was so worldly for to have offyce.

For him was lever have at his beddes heed
Twenty bokes, clad in blak or reed,
Of Aristotle and his philosophye,
Than robes riche, or fithele, or gay sautrye.
But al be that he was a philosophre,
Yet hadde he but litel gold in cofre ;
But all that he mighte of his freendes hente,
On bokes and on lerninge he it spente,
And bisily gan for the soules preye
Of hem that yaf him wher-with to scoleye.
Of studie took he most cure and most hede.
Noght o word spak he more than was nede,
And that was seyd in forme and reverence,
And short and quik, and ful of hy sentence.
Souninge in moral vertu was his speche,
And gladly wolde he lerne, and gladly teche.

With this may be set the dozen lines on the Ploughman :

With him ther was a Plowman, was his brother,
That hadde y-lad of dong ful many a fother,
A trewe swinker and a good was he,
Livinge in pees and parfit charitee.
God loved he best with al his hole herte
At alle tymes, thogh him gamed or smerte,
And thanne his neighbour right as himselve.
He wolde thresshe, and there-to dyke and delve,
For Cristes sake, for every povre wight,
Withouten hyre, if it lay in his might.
His tythes payed he ful faire and wel,
Both of his propre swink and his catel.
In a tabard he rood upon a mere.

Chaucer had an extraordinary facility in conveying a
sense of character by notes of personal appearance :

The Reeve was a sclendre colerick man,
His berd was shav as ny as ever he can . . .

in striking contrast to the Miller, who played them out
of town on their pilgrimage with his bagpipes, of whom
we hear—

> His berd as any sowe or fox was reed,
> And ther-to brood, as though it were a spede.

Four lines are enough to give us more than a nodding
acquaintance with the Summoner—

> A Somnour was ther with us in that place,
> That hadde a fyr-reed cherubinnes face,
> For sawcefleem he was, with eyen narwe.
> As hoot he was, and lecherous, as a sparwe ;

and in a few more we are on speaking terms with the
Pardoner :

> This pardoner hadde heer as yelow as wax,
> But smothe it heng, as dooth a strike of flex ;
> By ounces henge his lokkes that he hadde,
> And ther-with he his shuldres overspradde ;
> But thinne it lay, by colpons oon and oon ;
> But hood, for jolitee, ne wered he noon,
> For it was trussed up in his walet.
> Him thoughte, he rood al of the newe jet ;
> Dischevele, save his cappe, he rood al bare.
> Swiche glaringe eyen hadde he as an hare.

Even more remarkable is Chaucer's power of suggesting
character by a mere description of dress. If we knew
no more of the Wife of Bath than this, how well should
we know her still :

> Hir coverchiefs ful fyne were of ground ;
> I dorste swere they weyeden ten pound
> That on a Sonday were upon hir heed.
> Hir hosen weren of fyn scarlet reed,

Ful streite y-teyd, and shoos ful moiste and newe.
Bold was hir face, and fair, and reed of hewe.

. . . . . .

Up-on an amblere esily she sat,
Y-wimpled wel, and on hir heed an hat
As brood as is a bokeler or a targe ;
A foot-mantel aboute hir hipes large,
And on hir feet a paire of spores sharp.
In felawschip wel coude she laughe and carpe.

Single phrases that have become current in the language are rare in Chaucer.   The most famous, perhaps, is—

Thanne is it wisdom, as it thinketh me,
To maken vertu of necessitee,

which was borrowed in turn by Rabelais, Erasmus and Shakespeare.

The smyler with the knyf under the cloke

has, perhaps, hardly acquired the proverbial rank that he deserves, though a poor linguist may still sometimes be ridiculed for speaking French like the Prioress

After the scole of Stratford atte Bowe.

Nowhere in poetry is a man's fugitive state more poignantly summed than in—

Now with his love, now in his colde grave
Allone, with-outen any companye,

and an obvious word has seldom been invested with more surprise than in

Now have I dronke a draughte of corny ale.

6

A vivid little note from our earliest theatre survives in
the record of Absolom, the parish clerk, that

> Somtyme, to shewe his lightnesse and maistrye,
> He pleyeth Herodes on a scaffold bye,

and although in the lines

> Out of these blake wawes for to sayle,
> O wind, O wind, the wedder ginneth clere,

there is nothing above the common—and very high—
level of Chaucer, there is a note that was exactly caught
again five hundred years later by William Morris.

When the Man of Law is required by the Host to
make his contribution to the pilgrims' entertainment,
he says that he is very willing to do his best, but com-
plains that all the good tales have already been told in
one book or another by Chaucer except such ' unkinde
abhominaciouns ' as he too is unwilling to repeat.   The
poet's objective reference to himself in this passage is
quite foreign to his habit, and none the less significant
in consequence.   The Man of Law says :

> I can right now no thrifty tale seyn,
> But Chaucer, though he can but lewedly [unlearnedly]
> On metres and on ryming craftily,
> Hath seyd hem in swich English as he can . . .

and proceeds to give a rhymed hand-list of the poet's
work.   Chaucer's mild self-disparagement here, ob-
viously, need not be taken very seriously.   His unfailing
sense of dramatic propriety dictates the tone of an
allusion that must nevertheless have been made with
some purpose, and in view of Chaucer's special position
in English poetry, attention is claimed by any word

that may help us to know what he thought of himself.
At the end of his poem on Troilus and Cressida, written
in his middle period before *The Canterbury Tales,* and
running to over a thousand stanzas in rhyme royal, he
dedicates what was then his major work to Gower and
Strode, the latter a poet now lost in the mists of time.

> O moral Gower, this book I directe
> To thee, and to the philosophical Strode,
> To vouchen sauf, ther nede is, to corecte,
> Of your benignitees and zeles gode.

So far as is known, Gower was some fifteen years and
the nebulous Strode as much Chaucer's senior. Sub-
mission to their correction was a courtesy of the sort
that has graced literary annals as often as animosities
have disgraced them. We may believe that it was not
insincere, although in literal fact Chaucer would hardly
have welcomed even the moral Gower's interference
with his manuscripts—and it must be remembered that
manuscript publication was the only kind that Chaucer
knew. As it happens, we have his own explicit views
on the matter, also given at the end of the Troilus poem :

> And for ther is so great diversitee
> In English and in wryting of our tonge,
> So preye I God that noon miswryte thee, [his book]
> Ne thee mismêtre for defaute of tonge.
> And red wher-so thou be, or elles songe,
> That thou be understoude I God beseche !

So, we learn, Chaucer gently could profess himself un-
learned in verse, and pay respectful homage to the
superior judgement of his elder contemporaries, but he
had sufficient knowledge of his own merit to lay his
malediction on any one who should tamper with the

word as it came from his pen. Moreover, in that line
' ne thee mismetre for defaute of tonge ', following on
the remark about the transitional state of the English
language in his time, he shows an astonishingly prophetic
appreciation of the problems with which his genius was
coping in a manner altogether beyond the comprehen-
sion of any one else in his age. Saintsbury, in the centre
of the target as usual, writes : ' The old seventeenth
and eighteenth century notion that he could not scan
is, of course, now held by no instructed person.' But,
as Chaucer himself feared, he was much ' mismetred '
for long enough after his death. As late as 1810 Alex-
ander Chalmers, writing for his monumental edition
of the English poets, still felt it expedient to adopt a
defensive attitude. He could quote Johnson as saying
that Chaucer was ' the first of our versifiers who wrote
poetically ', and Thomas Warton, the first considerable
historian of English poetry, to the effect that ' in eleva-
tion and elegance, in harmony and perspicuity of versi-
fication, he surpasses his predecessors in an infinite pro-
portion '. Notwithstanding these opinions, however,
and the enlightenment with which Tyrwhitt thirty-five
years earlier had edited *The Canterbury Tales*, Chalmers,
who was no fool, could still write :

Although Chaucer has been generally hailed as the founder
of English poetry and literature, the extent of the obligations
which English poetry and literature owe to him has not been
decidedly ascertained. The improvement he introduced in
language and versification has been called in question, not
only by modern but by ancient critics. The chief faults
attributed to him are the mixture of French in all his works,
and his ignorance of the laws of versification.

Chalmers decidedly dissociated himself from these views,

but the passage indicates their prevalence even at so late a date. It was as Chaucer had foreseen. He realized that the experimental nature of his verse, supported by no previously established standards to which after ages could refer, would leave him open to the charge of technical insufficiency. The problem of future criticism was not to be the measuring of his verse to known authority, but the discovery of a secret that was his and his alone, a much more delicate matter. Knowing the difficulties with which his fame would have to contend, he might well contemplate himself wryly enough, employing ' swich English as he can ', and pray to be delivered from misrepresentation. It was more than seventy years after the poet's death that William Caxton honoured himself and Chaucer by making *The Canterbury Tales* one of the early publications of his press, though from a corrupt manuscript, for which he apologized in a new edition. When again a hundred years later English poetry was at the dawn of its Elizabethan splendour, the language of which Chaucer laid the foundations had since his time undergone no radical change but just enough of syllabic modification to throw his metrical principles out of gear for readers who had not an instinctive trick of making the necessary adjustment. To a certain extent the difficulty still remains, though, as Saintsbury says, no sensible person to-day attributes it to a defect of Chaucer's art. For myself, I find that I can read Chaucer's verse with ease, its structure line by line presenting none but a very occasional obstacle to my ear. But I should by no means care to read it aloud to an audience.

One thing in any case is certain : there is no fumbling in Chaucer's verse once we know its secret, and the poet himself was unquestionably aware of his own mastery. People to come might 'miswryte' or 'mis-metre' him, but even amid the 'diversitee' of English tongues in his time, he knew, he must have known, that he had given English verse a firm flexibility of shape altogether beyond anything that it had achieved before. With all its difficulties, we can read nine lines out of ten in his verse with an unhesitating perception of their cadence. His stock, almost his invariable measures are the four-foot and the five-foot iambic line. So far had any English practice in these before him been short of perfection or even competence, that it is hardly an exaggeration to say that he invented them. Since his example they have maintained unbroken supremacy through successive ages of English poetry. Contraction of the iambic line to less than eight syllables and expansion to more than ten have been used in many occasional successes, as have basically different measures, notably the anapest. But no form has been at all comparable in importance with the two that Chaucer originated and used with an effect that no later development could diminish. It was a stupendous performance. 'The morning star of song', as Tennyson called him, had no English masters to acknowledge but Gower and Strode, masters whom he had left far behind. But he could associate himself, humbly but confidently, with the great ones of an older world :

> Go, litel book, go litel myn tregedie,
> Ther god thy maker yet, er that he dye,
> So sende might to make in som comedie !
> But litel book, no making thou n'envye,
> But subgit be to alle poesye ;
> And kis the steppes, wher-as thou seest pace
> Virgile, Ovyde, Omer, Lucan, and Stace.

VII

POETRY AND NARRATIVE (2)

CHAUCER died in 1400. His appearance as a poet was phenomenal. If we can imagine English history as having for some reason come to an end in 1550, it would have been more phenomenal still. For then it would have appeared to after-time, if the records had been preserved, that the brilliant dawn of our poetry had been a false one, lapsing into a night from which there had been no recovery, and leaving Chaucer in solitary splendour as the one great poet of his race. For nearly a hundred and fifty years after his death, nothing was produced in English poetry that any one would miss to-day if it had not been written. If there were nothing else in the world to read, some of the verse romances of the fifteenth century might seem less tedious than they are, though I must confess that I have not read *Sir Launfal*, by Thomas Chester (who escapes even the fine mesh of the *Dictionary of National Biography*), a poem that Saintsbury found 'beautiful' in an age that even his enthusiasm allowed to be peopled by a 'vast army of dull versifiers'. Sir Launfal or no Sir Launfal, the poetry of the age did nothing whatever to fulfil the promise or even remotely to emulate the achievement of Chaucer. The English genius—Scotland had not yet joined us—turned instead to prose, and it was Thomas Malory's *Morte Arthur* that redeemed the century from creative sterility.

Chaucer first and last was a narrative poet, narrative, that is to say, in the specific sense as distinct from epic and dramatic, which themselves belong to narrative in the generic sense. For reasons which will be examined later, his example in this respect had a far smaller influence on the subsequent practice of English poetry than would have seemed likely to a shrewd critic of his own time. Chaucer himself apart, narrative poetry (specifically again) has taken a relatively unimportant place in our verse. Chaucer and, with a difference, Spenser, are the only English poets whose chief claim to their standing in the first rank is founded on their performance in this kind. The Elizabethans, Chaucer's first inheritors of consequence, gave it some attention, but they were mostly otherwise preoccupied. Before we come to them, however, there is something more to say about the fifteenth and early sixteenth centuries.

The main stream of literature always has many tributaries, some of them with sturdy currents of their own, some no more than trickling runnels or almost stagnant backwaters. But—to leave the metaphor—in most periods there is also another kind of activity that, illogically perhaps, hardly seems to relate itself in our minds to the main enterprise of literature at all. The music-hall songs of our own time are an example. Most of them are rubbish, but a few have merit which may some day delight the heart of an industrious editor. Nevertheless, apart from the intellectual pose that goes music-halling in much the same spirit as the young women of Mayfair go slumming, it does not occur to any one that they need serious consideration in the study of contemporary poetry. They are fugitive in occasion, they are not read, nobody troubles to preserve them, and for all that is known of their authors they might be anonymous.

In the fifteenth century there was a considerable body of verse that in circumstance, though not in quality, may be said to fall into this class. Chaucer was a deliberate literary artist, by which I mean that he wrote books, took what steps he could towards their preservation, would certainly have availed himself of the printing press if it had existed in his time, and speculated on their future reputation among readers. When he died, he had, in fact, set the main stream of poetry going on a very impressive tide. For a century after, as we have seen, the banks contracted and the tributaries were negligible. In the meantime, however, remarkable poetry was being written, or we might more fitly say made, by men who as likely as not knew nothing of Chaucer, and yet were far better poets than any of the successors who inherited but did nothing to honour his deliberately literary tradition.

Of these poets not a single name has survived. They were the authors of mystery, miracle and morality plays, ballads and carols. The drama, in priestly keeping, had been a part of religious ritual in England since the eleventh century, perhaps earlier. Through the fourteenth and fifteenth centuries it gathered secular significance, and Chaucer's Herod on a scaffold high was by this time a familiar figure of civic life. The trade guilds of York, Townely, Coventry, Chester and other towns wrote and acted their own cycles of plays, and at the end of the fifteenth century the genius of a long tradition culminated in the magnificent achievement of *Everyman*. These plays have a far greater vitality than their contemporary verse romances, they still can be lively enough when put on the stage, and in occasional passages they show touches of insight and imagination that faintly foretell the Elizabethan theatre. But on the whole their poetry is of minor importance beyond its original occasion, which it served admirably. It is interesting but not magnetic. The plays of the Greeks and the Elizabethans also need the stage for their full realization, but without it they would remain among the splendours of world literature and still be constantly read. Nothing of the sort can be claimed for our fourteenth- and fifteenth-century dramatic poets, genuine creators though they were.

The ballads are another matter. We need have nothing to do with the fantastic notion that they were by some unexplained process communal productions. A poem must be written by a poet, and that is all there is about it. These poems, surviving as they did from generation to generation by oral tradition alone, doubtless underwent many modifications in the process, but that has nothing to do with the question, which with rational people cannot be a question at all.

The ballad-mongers were survivals of an old tradition. Travelling with their own or borrowed verses to speak or sing, they picked up a living with no responsibilities. Their tales, either celebrating well-known events of history or epitomizing the interminable romances that the common man had neither time nor inclination to read, were welcome at any fireside. Beyond this sociable traditional use, however, no account was taken of these poems either by their authors or by their minstrels. They might well have disappeared into oblivion as the progress of printing put the English troubadour out of business, had not some unknown enthusiast of the early seventeenth century made a substantial collection of them in a manuscript folio which was recovered and printed by Bishop Percy in 1765. It is possible that this ballad poetry has shone with a brighter lustre on account of the prevailing gloom of its period, but nevertheless it contains a few of the loveliest short poems in the language. Sometimes the promise of a first-rate opening is not quite fulfilled, as in

> True Thomas lay on Huntlie bank,

and even, I think, in

> As ye came from the Holy Land
> Of Walsinghame,

though the whole movement in this is beautiful. The six short stanzas of *The Bonny Earl of Murray* just manage to live up to the opening magic of

> Ye Highlands and ye Lawlands,
> O where hae ye been? . . .

and 'There lived a wife at Usher's Well' gathers strength as it goes on, though I suspect some hiatus in the text at the conclusion. *Clerk Saunders* has a sepulchral power that, though sometimes it seems to be on the point of parodying itself, is used with masterly effect, and the same may be said, rather more doubtfully, of *Binnorie*. *Helen of Kirconnell* comes near to perfection ; *Waly, Waly*, and *Sir Patrick Spens* certainly achieve it. The opening of the last :

> The King sits in Dunfermline town
> Drinking the blude-red wine . . .

is among the unapproachable marvels of poetry, an apotheosis of the ballad genius in a phrase. But indeed the whole poem is a marvel, down to a close superbly worthy of the beginning :

> Half-owre, half-owre to Aberdour,
>   'Tis fifty fathoms deep ;
> And there lies gude Sir Patrick Spens,
>   Wi' the Scots lords at his feet !

Waly, Waly is strictly a ballad, but it is a ballad with a difference. *Sir Patrick Spens*, for me the crown of them all, is plain objective narrative. *Waly, Waly*, hardly below that or any level, is half-way over to pure subjective lyric, and in this it is, with certain other poems of the period, of high historic importance in poetry. *Sir Patrick Spens*, for all its greatness, could teach later poets nothing that, disregarding metrical considerations, they might not have learnt from Chaucer, but there is nothing in Chaucer comparable to the note of *Waly, Waly*. The poem is so much to our purpose here, that I will ask my readers, who are doubtless already familiar enough with it, to give themselves the pleasure of reading it again.

> O waly, waly, up the bank,
>   And waly, waly, doun the brae,
> And waly, waly, yon burn-side,
>   Where I and my Love wont to gae !
> I lean'd my back unto an aik,
>   I thocht it was a trustie tree ;
> But first it bow'd and syne it brak—
>   Sae my true love did lichtlie me.

> O waly, waly, gin love be bonnie
>   A little time while it is new !
> But when 'tis auld it waxeth cauld,
>   And fades awa' like morning dew.

O wherefore should I busk my heid,
   Or wherefore should I kame my hair ?
For my true Love has me forsook,
   And says he'll never lo'e me mair.

Now Arthur's Seat sall be my bed,
   The sheets sall ne'er be 'filed by me ;
Saint Anton's well sall be my drink ;
   Since my true Love has forsaken me.
Marti'mas wind, when wilt thou blaw,
   And shake the green leaves aff the tree ?
O gentle Death, when wilt thou come ?
   For of my life I am wearie.

'Tis not the frost, that freezes fell,
   Nor blawing snaw's inclemencie,
'Tis not sic cauld that makes me cry ;
   But my Love's heart grown cauld to me.
When we cam in by Glasgow toun,
   We were a comely sicht to see ;
My Love was clad in the black velvèt,
   And I mysel in cramasie.

But had I wist, before I kist,
   That love had been sae ill to win,
I had lock'd my heart in a case o' gowd,
   And pinn'd it wi' a siller pin.
And O ! if my young babe were born,
   And set upon the nurse's knee ;
And I mysel were dead and gane,
   And the green grass growing over me !

That, and a few—a very few—other things like it,
was on a small scale as new in English poetry as *The
Canterbury Tales* had been on a large. Of this lyric
self-consciousness, which was destined to be the source
of so much that we cherish, there was hardly a trace

in Chaucer. A tiny *ballade* and half a dozen casual allusions are about the sum of his lyric manifestations, and even these are mostly touched with a note of irony, as though he were a little ashamed of calling attention to himself. The poet of *Waly, Waly* is frankly unashamed of anything. It is a safe hazard, since authoritative contradiction is impossible, to suggest that the poet may have been a woman. In any case, she or he would have been congenial to the author of Shakespeare's sonnets, who, there is good reason to believe, was William Shakespeare.

Of the ballad poems that complete the transition of *Waly, Waly* from narrative to lyric, the most notable is *The Nut-Brown Maid*. If the fifteenth century had produced nothing but this rhymed dialogue, it would still not be without its title of honour in a great record. The poem has an enchanting ballad story, but the emotion is lyrical throughout. One stanza must serve as a reminder of its quality :

> *She.*   Though in the wood I understood
> Ye had a paramour,
> All this may nought remove my thought,
> But that I will be your' :
> And she shall find me soft and kind
> And courteis every hour ;
> Glad to fulfil all that she will
> Command me, to my power :
> For had ye, lo, an hundred mo,
> Yet would I be that one :
> For, in my mind, of all mankind
> I love but you alone.

The measure is that of *Sir Patrick Spens*, but the cunning management of the rhyme gives the twelve-line stanza an easy spaciousness that is very effective. It is odd

that so pleasing a form should not have been more
freely copied. In fact, although there may be later
poems in the same stanza, I can recall none ; certainly
there are not many. The light lyric movement of the
verse, however, is here, as in *Waly, Waly,* a hundred
years and more before its time, and it had not appeared
in English poetry before. And it is, indeed, not so
much to the Elizabethans as to the later cavalier lyrists
of the seventeenth century that it looks forward :

> Yet this inconstancy is such
>   As thou too shalt adore ;
> I could not love thee, Dear, so much,
>   Loved I not honour more.

That's the very thing. If Lovelace had not read *The
Nut-Brown Maid,* it's a wonder. A poem that throws
an even longer beam into the future, reminding us really
of no one before Coleridge, is *A Lyke-Wake Dirge,*
with another example of the great opening :

> This ae nighte, this ae nighte,
>   —*Every nighte and alle,*
> Fire and sleet and candle-lighte,
>   *And Christe receive thy saule.*

Before leaving the fifteenth century, let us show it with
one exquisite little poem that is just its own and nobody
else's :

CAROL

> I sing of a maiden
>   That is makeles ;
> King of all kings
>   To her son she ches.

He came al so still
  There his mother was,
As dew in April
  That falleth on the grass.

He came al so still
  To his mother's bour,
As dew in April
  That falleth on the flour.

He came al so still
  There his mother lay,
As dew in April
  That falleth on the spray.

Mother and maiden
  Was never none but she ;
Well may such a lady
  Goddes mother be.

Fifteenth-century lyric, however, though it can some-
times be as good as that, makes but a very small gather-
ing. The more prolific ballad and dramatic poets,
though they had little or no association with the master
Chaucer, followed him at least in making the adorn-
ment of a tale their ostensible motive, however much
they might point a moral in the process, which, it must
be said, was usually but little. And, again with Chaucer,
they usually succeed in giving their stories an interest
that holds our attention with ease. In their smaller
way they, like Chaucer, invest their poems with a larger
significance than that of the stories alone. *Sir Patrick
Spens* tells a very good but extremely simple story, but
if that were all it would not be the unforgettable thing
it is. And the transfiguring element is poetry, of which

the story is the occasion, the indispensable occasion it should be added. For Chaucer and these other specifically narrative poets, story was a deliberately chosen condition of their poetry. By it first and foremost they designed to hold us from play and the chimney corner, for whatever deeper purpose it might be. We ask ourselves again, how came it that this example was to be so little followed in the general development of English poetry?

First, we must distinguish a little more closely between the ballads and the plays of the fifteenth century. But as soon as we begin to do this we find that the essential distinction is in reality a very slender one. The plays are, in fact, much more like the ballads than they are like the crowded and complicated drama of the Elizabethans. It may almost be said that these early plays are neither more nor less than ballads made for acting. They have the same naïve simplicity of fable and character, and are hardly wider in intellectual scope. If these playwrights were the begetters of Marlowe and Shakespeare and Ben Jonson, it was on about the same scale as the yard-wide trickle at Lechlade to the Thames at London Bridge. On the other hand, if specific narrative as it appears in *The Canterbury Tales* had become a chief concern of English poetry, Chaucer, the source and first example, would have rivalled any of his posterity in stature. But it did not.

The first great English poem in point of time is *The Canterbury Tales*; the second is *The Fäerie Queen*. It was written in the years round about 1580, when Edmund Spenser was in his early thirties and Shakespeare still a boy; roughly speaking, two hundred years after the composition of Chaucer's masterpiece. It has superlative merits. The grace of its versification, sustained through nearly forty thousand lines, has never been excelled, and Spenser's invention of his stanza was a technical feat of inspired grandeur. His best editor, Ernest de Selincourt, says justly : ' Wordsworth and Keats have written lines which might have come from the pen of Milton ; no one has ever written a stanza that could be taken for Spenser's.' One celebrated passage may be given in illustration of this unexampled and unequalled union of strength and sweetness, and of Spenser's genius in its highest exercise :

The joyous birdes shrouded in chearefull shade,
Their notes unto the voyce attempred sweet ;
Th' Angelicall soft trembling voyces made
To th' instruments diuine respondence meet :
The siluer sounding instruments did meet
With the base murmure of the waters fall :
The waters fall with difference discreet,
Now soft, now loud, vnto the wind did call :
The gentle warbling wind low answered to all.

There, whence that Musick seemed heard to bee,
Was the faire Witch her selfe now solacing,
With a new Louer, whom through sorceree
And witchcraft, she from farre did thither bring :
There she had him now layd a slombering,
In secret shade, after long wanton ioyes :
Whilst round about them pleasauntly did sing
Many faire Ladies, and lasciuious boyes,
That euer mixt their song with light licentious toyes.

And all that while, right ouer him she hong,
With her false eyes fast fixed in his sight,
As seeking medicine, whence she was stong,
Or greedily depasturing delight :

And oft inclining downe with kisses light,
For feare of waking him, his lips bedewd,
And through his humid eyes did sucke his spright,
Quite molten into lust and pleasure lewd ;
Wherewith she sighed soft, as if his case she rewd.

The whiles some one did chaunt this louely lay ;
Ah see, who so faire thing doest faine to see,
In springing flowre the image of thy day ;
Ah see the Virgin Rose, how sweetly shee
Doth first peepe forth with bashful modestee,
That fairer seemes, the lesse ye see her may ;
Lo see soone after, how more bold and free
Her bared bosome she doth broad display ;
Loe see soone after, how she fades, and falles away.

So passeth, in the passing of a day,
Of mortall life the leafe, the bud, the flowre,
Ne more doth flourish after first decay,
That earst was sought to decke both bed and bowre,
Of many a Ladie, and many a Paramowre :
Gather therefore the Rose, whilest yet is prime,
For soone comes age, that will her pride deflowre :
Gather the Rose of loue, whilest yet is time,
Whilst louing thou mayst loued be with equall crime.

It is, however, the question of *The Fäerie Queen* as narrative that we are now considering. It is specifically a narrative poem. It tells a story, and it is certainly not an epic as it is not a drama. The story is deeply involved in allegory, sometimes, we may think, almost smothered by it, but it is a story none the less. And yet, for me at any rate, it is a story that entirely fails to hold the attention in the way that it is held by Chaucer. In these matters it is a case of every man to his own mind, and while I never find myself in disagreement with

Saintsbury without misgiving, I am at a loss to follow him when he says, ' *The Fäerie Queen*, more than almost any other poem, demands and deserves to be read as a whole if its full charm is to be comprehended and enjoyed.' I can only say that it is not my own experience. I can open it at any page and read a few stanzas with delighted admiration, but to follow the tenuous narrative thread of the poem for any considerable time is an effort that soon ceases to give me the finer pleasure of poetry. It seems to me, indeed, that Spenser's narrative instead of effecting the purpose for which narrative was so well used by Chaucer, exactly defeats it. Chaucer so uses a simple story as to engage our superficial attention while his poetry steals gently on the senses, taking possession of the soul. Spenser's story, on the other hand, so involved and diffuse and often obscure, demands a constant effort of the attention that should be easily and almost unconsciously employed, and is thus an impediment to the profounder reception of his poetry. In his excellent little book on the Epic, Mr. Lascelles Abercrombie writes words which I cannot refrain from setting beside Saintsbury's :

Not only because Spenser does not tell his stories very well, but even more because their substance (not, of course, their meaning) is deliciously and deliberately unreal, *The Faery Queene* is outside the strict sense of the word epic. Allegory requires material ingeniously manipulated and fantastic ; what is more important, it requires material invented by the poet himself. That is a long way from the solid reality of material which epic requires. Not manipulation, but imaginative transfiguration of material ; not invention, but selection of existing material appropriate to his genius, and complete absorption of it into his being ; that is how the epic poet works.

I shall borrow that again for later reference, but one sentence is precisely apt to my present purpose : ' Spenser does not tell his stories very well.' A narrative poem of great length that does not tell its story very well may on other accounts still be a great poem, but it must be an imperfect one, and that I think is the case with *The Fäerie Queen*. I do not mean flawless, but imperfection of an organic kind. *The Canterbury Tales* is far from being flawless, but it is organically sound. *The Fäerie Queen* abounds in beauties that were beyond the reach even of Chaucer, but the effect of the whole is seriously impaired by a structural looseness that seems to have derived rather from the abortive verse romances of the fifteenth century than from Chaucer. It is perhaps an equivocal, but not impertinent, measure of Spenser's genius that in spite of this *The Fäerie Queen* does remain a great poem, and could never be mistaken for anything else. But as narrative it is not greatly in the line of Chaucer, and in that respect takes the older poet's art to no new heights. As a poet Spenser is Chaucer's peer, the first in succession ; spiritually he has a range beyond Chaucer's, and this is shown as clearly in his shorter poems as in *The Fäerie Queen* ; but in the control of narrative Chaucer easily excels him.

Spenser was born in 1552. The early years of the following decade saw the birth of four other poets who did something to make it appear that narrative might become one of the staples of English poetry : Samuel Daniel in 1562, Michael Drayton in 1563, Christopher Marlowe and William Shakespeare in 1564.

The most originating force among these—which, it need hardly be added, is not to say that he was the most original poet—was Marlowe. Daniel and Drayton indeed, admirable poets though they were, hardly come into the reckoning. They belonged, with high honours, to the Elizabethan age, but they did little or nothing towards the direction of an energy from which they drew so deeply. Shakespeare, on the other hand, was the decisive genius who gave that energy its greatest and most durable form, and the influence of Marlowe on Shakespeare can hardly be exaggerated. Speculation as to what Marlowe would have done had he not come to a tragic end before he was thirty is futile, but there is no doubt that in the few years of his working life he realized the dawning splendour of the age with a sensuous gusto and a power of phrase which till then were his alone, and that this onset profoundly impressed the mind of his young and even more highly gifted contemporary. There is a strange analogy between the story of these two men and that of two of England's greatest painters two hundred years later. Thomas Girtin and J. M. W. Turner also were born in a year, 1775. Girtin, like Marlowe, died before he was thirty, leaving Turner, who had worked year by year at his side, to declare that had his friend lived he would himself have been eclipsed. This was an obituary exaggeration, but Turner in the days of his acknowledged greatness never forgot what his young genius owed to Girtin's. And if Shakespeare in the full maturity of his powers was ever asked to say what literary influence had most deeply affected him, we may surmise pretty confidently that Christopher Marlowe was the answer.

When Marlowe died in 1593 he left an unfinished narrative poem on Hero and Leander. It was later completed, indifferently well, by George Chapman, but

can be considered only as a fragment. There is enough
of it to show that Marlowe was potentially a master of
the form. In any passage we can see the assured design
and control. The story is perfectly suited to the pur-
poses of his poetry, and to the service of those purposes
it is firmly kept. We are eager to know from line to
line what is happening to these lovers, and while our
attention is so engaged our imagination is spell-bound
by a full-throated passion such as English poetry had
not yet known :

> For know, that underneath this radiant flour
> Was Danäe's statue in a brazen tower ;
> Jove slyly stealing from his sister's bed,
> To dally with Idalian Ganymed,
> And for his love Europa bellowing loud,
> And tumbling with the Rainbow in a cloud ;
> Blood-quaffing Mars heaving the iron net
> Which limping Vulcan and his Cyclops set ;
> Love kindling fire, to burn such towns as Troy ;
> Silvanus weeping for the lovely boy
> That now is turn'd into a cypress-tree,
> Under whose shade the wood-gods love to be.
> And in the midst a silver altar stood :
> There Hero, sacrificing turtle's blood,
> Vail'd to the ground, veiling her eyelids close ;
> And modestly they open'd as she rose :
> Thence flew Love's arrow with the golden head ;
> And thus Leander was enamourèd.
> Stone-still he stood, and evermore he gaz'd,
> Till with the fire, that from his countenance blaz'd,
> Relenting Hero's gentle heart was strook :
> Such force and virtue hath an amorous look.

Well indeed might Bradley say—and well indeed he
said it—'his soul seems to be in his eyes.' And when

a philosophical turn is taken, the poetry loses none of its force :

> It lies not in our power to love or hate,
> For will in us is over-rul'd by fate.
> When two are stript long e'er the course begin,
> We wish that one should lose, the other win ;
> And one especially do we affect
> Of two gold ingots, like in each respect :
> The reason no man knows ; let it suffice,
> What we behold is censur'd by our eyes.
> Where both deliberate, the love is slight :
> Who ever lov'd, that lov'd not at first sight ?

The highest praise that can be given to Shakespeare's *Venus and Adonis* is that it is the equal of *Hero and Leander*, and no praise could be higher. In some respects Shakespeare was already above Marlowe, or any one else. The mastery of diction, which was to become not only above all rivalry, but in his greatest plays an integral part of the drama itself, was even in these early years making history.

> Still she entreats, and prettily entreats,
> For to a pretty ear she tunes her tale :
> Still is he sullen, still he low'rs and frets,
> 'Twixt crimson shame and anger ashy pale :
>   Being red, she loves him best ; and being white,
>   Her best is bettered with a more delight.

That, to put it simply, is beyond anybody but Shakespeare as mere writing. His story, too, is unfailing in its interest, and none the less so in that its interest is largely of a kind that may excite anybody. Once and again there is perhaps a touch of self-assurance that is disconcerting, as in—

An oven that is stopp'd, or river stay'd,
Burneth more hotly, swelleth with more rage ;
So of conceal`è`d sorrow may be said,
Free vent of words love's fire doth assuage ;
But when the heart's attorney once is mute,
The client breaks, as desperate in his suit.

Again, nobody but Shakespeare could have written it,
but may we in our low estate ask whether he did not
write it just to show that he could ? And is not this
perhaps true of even the famous descriptive passages, as
that of the horse :

Imperiously he leaps, he neighs, he bounds,
And now his woven girth he breaks asunder ;
The bearing earth with his hard hoof he wounds,
Whose hollow womb resounds like heaven's thunder ;
The iron bit he crushes 'tween his teeth,
Controlling what he was controlled with.

His ears up-prick'd : his braided hanging mane
Upon his compass'd crest now stand on end ;
His nostrils drink the air, and forth again,
As from a furnace, vapours doth he send :
His eye, which scornfully glisters like fire,
Shows his hot courage and his high desire.

That is fine enough in all conscience, but does not even
it seem a little laboured when set beside, say, ' Still
she entreats, and prettily entreats ' ? This, however, is
quibbling in the presence. *Venus and Adonis* would
have put Shakespeare very near to the top of poetry
even if he had written nothing else, and that is enough.
But, even so, there is one essential quality in which it
just, or so I think, falls short of *Hero and Leander*. To
the passion of an age, which both poets shared with

no one else, Marlowe adds a note of personal passion more authentic than Shakespeare's. *Venus and Adonis* and *Hero and Leander* are both love poems, and Shakespeare *knew* as much about love as Marlowe. In the longer life that was given to him he was to search this knowledge with an insight that was beyond Marlowe's years. But in these two poems it is Marlowe who shows the more authoritatively that he not only knew about the passion of love but felt it as well. He gets nearer to the hearts of his lovers than Shakespeare does to the hearts of his. As we read the two lovely things, altogether above comparison in their own or any time, we feel that while Shakespeare is observing his Adonis with an inspired analytical insight, Marlowe would readily have leapt into the Hellespont with his Leander.

The only other poem to be put with *Hero and Leander* and *Venus and Adonis*, Shakespeare's own *Rape of Lucrece*, adds nothing to the argument. With these poems Marlowe and Shakespeare proved themselves capable of anything in the specific narrative that Chaucer had given to poetry. And with these, they left it, Shakespeare for the composition of forty plays, Marlowe for half a dozen and untimely death.

If it may be said that the story of *The Fäerie Queen* is a somewhat spineless backbone for the magnificent poetry that it is intended to support, conversely the story of Samuel Daniel's *History of the Civil War* is industriously and not quite uninterestingly told, but strangely it supports hardly any poetry at all. Strangely, because Daniel in other work, most notably the *Sonnets to Delia*, was a delightful poet, but when at the opening of his long narrative he wrote—

Come sacred Virtue ; I no Muse, but thee
Invoke, in this great labour I intend—

the Muse seems to have taken offence and left Virtue
severely to the job. Though the story of Richard and
Bolingbroke is told in generous but firm detail, it
obstinately refuses to fire or lighten into poetry. The
verse, which Daniel elsewhere uses so well, is steadily
pedestrian, and forces us to the conclusion that the tale
would have been better told in prose.[1] It is unaccount-
able. Considering the tenacity with which Daniel sticks
to his task, we cannot but believe that he had his heart
in it, and yet it reminds us of nothing so much as the
drearier wastes of the eighteenth century. Nothing of the
Elizabethan spirit is in it, and yet Daniel could write—

These plaintive verse, the posts of my desire,
Which hast for succour to her slow regard,
Bear not report of any slender fire ;
Forging a grief, to win a fame's reward.
Nor are my passions limn'd for outward hue,
For that no colours can depaint my sorrows :
Delia herself, and all the world may view
Best in my face, where cares have till'd deep furrows.
No bays I seek to deck my mourning brow,
O clear-ey'd rector of the holy hill !
My humble accents bear the olive bough
Of intercession, but to move her will.
These lines I use, t'unburthen mine own heart ;
My love affects no fame, nor steams of art,

---

[1] By the oddest coincidence, shortly after writing this I came across
these lines by Drayton, which I certainly do not remember having
read before. They are in a poetical epistle on ' Poets and Poesy ' :

Amongst these Samuel Daniel, whom if I
May speak of, but to censure do deny,
Only have heard some wise men him rehearse
To be too much historian in verse ;
His rhymes were smooth, his metres well did close,
But yet his manner better fitted prose.

which, but for two doubtful phrases, is perfect, and has one line that Vaughan or Crashaw might have inherited from Shakespeare ; and—

> Care-charmer Sleep, son of the sable Night ;
> Brother to Death, in silent darkness born :
> Relieve my languish, and restore the light ;
> With dark forgetting of my care, return.
> And let the day be time enough to mourn
> The shipwreck of my ill-adventur'd youth :
> Let waking eyes suffice to wail their scorn,
> Without the torment of the night's untruth.
> Cease, dreams, the images of day-desires,
> To model forth the passions of the morrow ;
> Never let rising Sun approve you liars,
> To add more grief to aggravate my sorrow.
> Still let me sleep, embracing clouds in vain ;
> And never wake to feel the day's disdain.

The only surviving interest of *The Civil Wars* is the further evidence it affords that the Elizabethan poets thought it worth while to spend a good deal of their time and energy on the specifically narrative form.

Much the same thing may be said of Michael Drayton's *Barons' Wars*, another long chronicle in verse, and in general a good deal below his usual level. It is in the same stanza as Daniel's poem, and it has a similar historical scheme. Also it makes a dangerous approach to the same flatness, though Drayton does contrive to give a little more impetus to his verse, enough to make us feel that it might at any moment break out into the real note. But it hardly ever does, and Drayton's principal narrative effort can be placed only a little above Daniel's, which is to say that as a living poem

to-day it is as near as no matter negligible. It remains
an interesting symptom, and that is all. Yet Drayton,
one of the most prolific poets of his age, had moments
when he was one of the best.

Since there's no help, come let us kiss and part—
Nay, I have done, you get no more of me ;
And I am glad, yea, glad with all my heart,
That thus so cleanly I myself can free.
Shake hands for ever, cancel all our vows,
And when we meet at any time again,
Be it not seen in either of our brows
That we one jot of former love retain.
Now at the last gasp of Love's latest breath,
When, his pulse failing, Passion speechless lies,
When Faith is kneeling by his bed of death,
And innocence is closing up his eyes,
 —Now if thou wouldst, when all have given him over,
 From death to life thou might'st him yet recover.

His shorter Agincourt poem, ' Fair stood the wind for
France ', is high among the few really first-rate heroic
lyrics in the language, and *Nymphidia* is at least an
astonishing *tour de force* without ever being tiresome.
If any one likes to read a topographical epic of fifteen
thousand lines—and six-foot lines at that—accompanied
by a prose commentary of some hundred thousand words,
Poly-Olbion awaits him with many curious and lovely
passages, though the most remarkable thing about the
poem must be that it should have been written at all.
But Drayton did an extraordinary variety of things in
poetry extraordinarily, if only now and then supremely
well, and although some say he was a quarrelsome
fellow, he kept a pleasant grace about himself in his
verse :

> And why not I, as he
> That's greatest, if as free,
>   In sundry strains that strive
> Since there so many be,
>   Th'old lyric kind revive ?

> I will, yea, and I may ;
> Who shall oppose my way ?
>   For what is he alone,
> That of himself can say
>   He's heir of Helicon.

And it is but fair to add that in some of his short narrative poems, those of a biblical origin for example, he does much better than in *The Barons' Wars*.

There is one other long narrative poem of the Spenserian or early Shakespearean period that claims attention. William Warner is a name but little known, and is not even mentioned in Courthope's exhaustive history. Nevertheless his *Albion's England* has merits which are not to be found in the corresponding work of greater men. It is a discursive history of England from the earliest times down to the poet's own. Written in rhymed ' fourteeners ', it runs to ten thousand lines or so, and as a whole it is insufficiently interesting in material to make it easy or even possible to read. But to look over its pages with an alert eye is to be arrested from time to time by quite surprising beauties. Drayton in his epistle wrote :

> Then Warner, tho' his lines were not so trimm'd,
> Nor yet his poem so exactly limn'd
> And neatly jointed, but the critic may
> Easily reprove him, yet thus let me say :

For my old friend, some passages there be
In him, which I protest have taken me
With almost wonder, so fine, clear, and new,
As yet they have been equalled by few.

'Have taken me with almost wonder'—that was
generous of Drayton, but no more than just. For
Warner has passages in which the 'wonder' of poetry
is unmistakably present, as it never is present in Daniel's
Civil Wars or Drayton's own *Barons' Wars*. Even in
the duller part of the poem, that is to say in most of it,
Warner uses his fourteeners with a rather fine swagger,
and you never know when he will turn up with some-
thing remarkable, such as—

Had one man all that all men have, he nothing had, unlesse
He also had a soule that all as nothing did possesse.

And sometimes he keeps it up for a considerable stretch
at a time. The pastoral interlude of Curan and Argentile
is a complete story in itself, and lovely. So little is it
known, that I should like to give its hundred and fifty
lines in full, but a brief example of its quality must
serve. Curan, a prince, falls in love with Argentile, a
princess, unsuccessfully. Retiring to a shepherd's life,
he consoles himself with the charms of a 'neatheard's
maid', who is, with traditional propriety, none other
than Argentile herself. As he woos, he begins to talk
of her whom he had loved and lost. In the convention,
Argentile is unknown to him, but as she recognizes
herself in his description she penetrates his disguise,
exclaiming :

thy latter speech bewraies
Thy clownish shape a coinèd show,

declares herself, and all is well. He is telling her why
she should choose a shepherd for a husband :

' Then chuse a shepheard. With the Sun he doth his flocke
    unfold,
And all the day on hill or plaine he merrie chat can hold :

And with the Sun doth folde againe ; then jogging home
    betime,
He turns a crab, or tunes a round, or sings some merrie
    ryme :

Nor lackes he gleeful tales to tell, whilst round the bole
    doth trot ;
And sitteth singing care away, till he to bed hath got.

There sleepes he soundly all the night, forgetting morrow
    cares,
Nor feares he blasting of his corne nor uttering of his wares,

Or stormes by seas, or stirres on land, or cracke of credite
    lost,
Not spending franklier than his flocke shall still defray the
    cost.

Wel wot I, sooth they say that say : more quiet nightes and
    daies
The shepheard sleepes and wakes than he whose cattel he
    doth graize.

Beleeve me lasse, a king is but a man, and so am I ;
Content is worth a monarchie, and mischiefes hit the hie :

As late it did a king and his, not dwelling far from hence,
Who left a daughter, (save thy selfe) for faire a matchlesse
    wench : '
(Here did he pause, as if his tongue had done his heart offence.)

The neatresse, longing for the rest, did egge him on to tell
How faire she was, and who she was. ' She bore,' quoth
   he, ' the bell

For beautie : though I clownish am, I know what beautie is,
Or did I not, yeat seeing thee, I senceless were to mis.

Suppose her beautie Hellen's-like, or Hellen's somewhat lesse,
And every starre consorting to a puer complexion gesse.

Her stature comely tall, her gate well graced, and her wit
To marvell at, not meddle with, as matchless I omit.

   .   .   .   .

A quiet mind, a patient mood, and not disdaining any :
Not gybing, gadding, gawdie, and her faculties were many.

A nimph, no tong, no heart, no eie, might praise, might
   wish, might see
For life, for love, for forme, more good, more worth, more
   faire, then she :

Yea such an one, as such was none, save only she was such :
Of Argentile to say the most were to be silent much.'

   When all is said, however, and even with Spenser in
the reckoning, Elizabethan and Jacobean poetry would
not be sensibly diminished in stature if deprived of its
specific narrative. Its supremacy rests on the drama
and lyric, and although the poets could then, to quote
Drayton again, pay their duties to ' that noble Chaucer '
who

               in those former times,
   The first enrich'd our English with his rhymes,
   And was the first of ours that ever brake
   Into the Muses' treasure, and first spake
   In weighty numbers, delving in the mine
   Of perfect knowledge, which he could refine,

8

And coin for current, and as much as then
The English language could express to men,
He made it do ; and by his wondrous skill,
Gave us much light from his abundant quill,

they mostly disregarded his instruction. His technical discoveries were not wasted in their practice, but they put their practice to other ends than his. Moreover, nothing of major importance happened in specifically narrative poetry for a hundred years and more after them. They applied their genius chiefly to dramatic and lyric poetry. During the decline of the drama through the seventeenth century, lyric held its own, and even enlarged its territory. Many specifically narrative poems were written, some of them engaging and none of them necessary. But narrative in another form appeared. Milton wrote the only true epic in the language, and took his place with Shakespeare among the seven—or ten if you will—supreme poets of the world.

Chaucer, then *The Fäerie Queen* and three middle-flights in length, though not in genius, by Marlowe and Shakespeare, and then again nothing in Chaucer's kind until the appearance of that god-like waif of literature, Oliver Goldsmith. *The Deserted Village*, published in 1770, is deservedly a very popular poem. But it is more than that. It is a recovery, against all the odds, of a secret that Chaucer first revealed, that the Elizabethans saluted with their omniscience in passing, and that then waited for nearly two hundred years on the casual summons of an Irish vagrant. And now we may go back on our tracks, leaving the ' specific narrative ', of which term the reader may very well—though unavoidably—by this time be tired, and see how poetry in its younger days moved in lyric and drama.

VIII

EARLY LYRIC

IT is well sometimes to remind ourselves that all our
critical distinctions between one kind of poetry and
another are ultimately artificial and made only for our
own intellectual convenience. Poetry is poetry, and
its essence remains unchanged through all its mani-
festations. The sacred fire that burns in *The Canterbury
Tales* burns also in *Macbeth* and *Paradise Lost* and *The
Prelude* ; but it burns too in *Waly, Waly*, and ' Since
there's no help, come let us kiss and part ', and the *Ode
to a Nightingale,* and ' O my Luve's like a red, red rose '.
Our distinctions can be serviceable enough, so long as
we make them with a due sense of their nature and of
their danger.

Remembering then that the poet's first concern is
the creation of poetry, and that in this he is by himself
alone, no matter what form the poetry may take, it
may be allowed that outside this basic condition of
creation the poet will be influenced by one of two con-
siderations. Either he will, in the final organization of
the thing that he has created, take an audience into
account, in which case some form of narrative—i.e. epic,
drama, or our ' specific narrative '—will be the result ;
or he will be unconscious of or indifferent to this element,

in which case he will employ the more personal, or perhaps we should say rather, the more private expression of lyric. In both cases his responsibility to poetry is the same, but in the former case he acknowledges also a social responsibility which does not affect his calculations in the latter.

Mankind's primitive desire for a story probably accounts for the fact that the recorded poetry of early periods usually takes some form of narrative. I say recorded since, using Chaucer as our example, it seems to me not improbable and certainly not impossible that a poet in his circumstances may have written lyrics for his own satisfaction but have given them no public circulation, supposing them to be of no public interest. The two or three of his lyrics that do survive, for example—

> Your yën two wol slee me sodenly,
> I may the beautè of hem not sustene,
> So woundeth hit through-out my herte kene.
>
> And but your word wol helen hastily
> My hertes wounde, whyl that hit is grene,
> *Your yën two wol slee me sodenly,*
> *I may the beautè of hem not sustene.*
>
> Upon my trouthe I sey yow feithfully,
> That ye ben of my lyf and deeth the quene;
> For with my deeth the trouthe shal be sene.
> *Your yën two wol slee me sodenly,*
> *I may the beautè of hem not sustene,*
> *So woundeth hit through-out my herte kene,*

though they are no more than happy exercises in a foreign manner, show what he could have done in the lyric if he had chosen. As it is, the purely personal lyric has no place in his very substantial body of work, nor does it come with any prevalence into English poetry until a hundred and fifty years after his death. It is true that even before his time, as early perhaps as the mid-thirteenth century, a few lyrics English in character though still transitional in language were being written, of which the Cuckoo Song is the most celebrated, and as good as any :

> Sumer is icumen in,
>   Lhude sing cuccu !
> Groweth sed, and bloweth med,
>   And springth the wude nu—
>   Sing cuccu !

> Awe bleteth after lomb,
>   Lhouth after calve cu :
> Bulluc sterteth, bucke verteth,
>   Murie sing cuccu !

> Cuccu, cuccu, well singes thu, cuccu :
>   Ne swike thu naver nu ;
> Sing cuccu, nu, sing cuccu,
>   Sing cuccu, sing cuccu, nu !

There is a cheerful fragrance in its single note, and in such a poem as ' Wynter wakeneth al my care ', written perhaps about 1300, there is a sharpening of emotion that looks forward to the carols of the ballad era. It is not, however, until we come to Sir Thomas Wyatt in the first half of the sixteenth century that we find English lyric fairly under way. And then, in one poem at least, we hear for the first time a strain that was destined to enrich generations of song. Familiar as it is, it is too important both for its own sake and historically not to be given in full :

THE LOVER COMPLAINETH THE UNKINDNESS OF
HIS LOVE

My lute awake perform the last
Labour, that thou and I shall wast :
And end that I have now begonne,
And when this song is song and past,
My lute be still for I have done.

As to be heard where eare is none,
As leade to grave in marble stone ;
My song may pearse her hart as sone.
Should we then sigh, or sing, or mone,
No, no, my lute, for I have done.

The rockes do not so cruelly
Repulse the waves continually,
As she my sute and affection :
So that I am past remedy,
Whereby my lute and I have done.

Proude of the spoile that thou hast gotte
Of simple harts through loves shot,
By whome unkind thou hast them wonne :
Think not he hath his bow forgot ;
Although my lute and I have done.

Vengeance shall fall on thy disdaine
That makest but game on earnest payne,
Think not alone under the sunne
Unquit to cause thy lovers plaine ;
Although my lute and I have done.

May chance thee lie withered and olde,
In winter nightes that are so colde,
Playning in vaine unto the mone ;
Thy wishes then dare not be tolde :
Care then who list, for I have done.

And then may chaunce thee to repent
The time that thou hast lost and spent,
To cause thy lovers sighe and swowne ;
Then shalt thou know beautie but lent,
And wish and want as I have done.

Now cease, my lute, this is the last
Labour, that thou and I shall wast,
And ended is that we begonne :
Now is this song both song and past ;
My lute be still, for I have done.

Wyatt was born in 1503, and died at the age of thirty-
nine. His poems were not printed until 1557, when
they appeared with the work of other authors in *Tottel's
Miscellany*, the publication of which was to be a land-
mark for ever in the progression of English poetry.
'Awake my Lute' is Wyatt's best poem, but nearly
almost all his lyrics, of which love is the constant theme,
have touches of the same quality. Moreover, he and
his friend Henry Howard, Earl of Surrey, who was fifteen
years his junior and shared with him the chief honours
of Tottel's collection, introduced the sonnet into England.
These men were poets of about equal endowment, but
the younger took the technical management of verse a
step farther than his master, and added another degree
of stability to the still tentative principles of diction.
Here is a sonnet by Wyatt :

Unstable dreame, according to the place,
Be stedfast ones, or els at least be true ;
By tasted swetnesse, make me not to rew
The sodeyn losse of thy false fayned grace.
By good respect in such a dangerous case,
Thou broughtest not her into these tossing seas ;
But madest my sprite to live, my care t'encrease,
My body in tempest her delight t'embrace,
The body dead, the sprite had his desire,
Painless was th'one, the other in delight.
Why then, alas ! did it not kepe it right,
But thus returne to leape into the fier ;
    And where it was at wish, could not remaine ?
    Such mockes of dreames do turn to deadly payne.

And here one by Surrey :

Set me whereas the sunne both parche the grene,
Or where his beames do not dissolve the yse :
In temperate heate where he is felt and sene :
In presence prest of people madde or wise :
Set me in hye, or yet in low degree ;
In longest night, or in the shortest daye :
In clearest skie, or where cloudes thickest be ;
In lusty youth, or when my heeres are graye :
Set me in heaven, in earth, or els in hell,
In hyll or dale, or in the foming flood,
Thrall, or at large, alive whereso I dwell,
Sicke or in health, in evill fame or good :
Hers will I be, and onely with this thought
Content my self, although my chaunce be nought.

Poetry apart, Surrey's advance in technical assurance is
clear. Another generation was to pass before the final
mastery was reached in Shakespeare and other great
though lesser men of his time, but already in the early
middle century the poets of *Tottel's Miscellany* were

authoritatively heralding the new age. Such verse as
this by Surrey, unassuming as it is, was without example
in English when he wrote it, but was itself an example
of endless promise :

> Martiall, the things that doe attain
> The happy life, be these I finde,
> The riches left, not got with pain ;
> The fruitfull ground, the quiet minde,
> The egall frend ; no grudge, no strife ;
> No charge of rule, nor governaunce ;
> Without disease, the healthful life ;
> The houshold of continuance :
> The meane dyet, no delicate fare ;
> Trew wisedome joynde with simplenesse ;
> The night discharged of all care ;
> Where wine the witte may not oppresse.
> The faithfull wife, without debate ;
> Such slepes as may begile the night ;
> Contented with thine owne estate,
> Ne wish for death, ne feare his might.

The poems of now uncertain authorship included by
Tottel in his *Miscellany* leave Wyatt and Surrey in com-
mand, but a few have decided claims of their own.
This is charming in any case, and, having been written
before 1550, remarkable.

THE LOVER IN LIBERTY SMILETH AT THEM IN THRALDOME, THAT SOMETIME SCORNED HIS BONDAGE

> At libertie I sit and see
> Them that have earst laught me to scorne,
> Whipt with the whip that scourged me,
> And now they banne that they were borne.

I see them sit full sobrelye
And think their earnest lokes to hide :
Now in themselves they cannot spye,
That they or this in me have spide.

I see them sitting al alone,
Marking the steppes, ech worde and loke,
And now they treade where I have gone
The painful pathe that I forsoke.

Now I see well, I saw no whit
When they saw well that now are blinde ;
But happy hap hath made me quit,
And just judgment hath them asinde.

I see them wander al alone,
And treade full fast in dredfull dout,
The selfe same path that I have gone :
Blessed be hap that brought me out.

At libertie all this I see,
And say no word but earst among,
Smiling at them that laught at me,
Lo such is hap, marke well my song.

That is better than the work of Nicholas Grimald,
another contributor to the volume, whom Warton
mistakenly declared to be Surrey's equal.   Though even
Grimald was doing something for the cause.

Philip Sidney was born in 1554, three years before
the appearance of Tottel's book.   Neither Wyatt nor
Surrey lived to see their poems in print, the former
having died in 1542, and Surrey having been murdered
on the block by Henry the Eighth, a few days before
that whimsical monarch, in Saintsbury's pleasing words,

' went to his own place'. By the time Sidney was a
young man, the Elizabethan throne had established
itself. In the meanwhile, working in succession to
Wyatt and Surrey were three or four poets of whom
brief mention must be made. George Gascoigne, born
in 1625, is the sort of poet who if he had been ten per
cent would have been a hundred per cent better. In
most of the things he wrote there is a notable talent
labouring for release, but the labour commonly overlays
the talent. In just one poem, however, and I do not
find another to set beside it, he did get clear of the
shackles, and the result is altogether charming :

> Sing lullaby, as women doe,
> Wherewith they bring their babes to rest,
> And lullaby can I sing to,
> As womanly as can the best.
> With lullaby they still the childe,
> And if I be not much beguild,
> Full many wanton babes have I,
> Which must be stild with lullabie.

> First lullaby my youthfull yeares,
> It is nowe time to go to bed,
> For croocked age and hoary heares,
> Have wone the haven with in my head :
> With Lullaby then youth be still,
> With Lullaby content thy will,
> Since courage quayles, and commes behind,
> Go sleepe, and so beguile thy minde.

> Next Lullaby my gazing eyes,
> Which wonted were to glaunce apace.
> For every Glasse maye nowe suffise,
> To shewe the furrowes in my face :

With Lullabye then winke awhile,
With Lullabye your lookes beguile :
Lette no fayre face, nor beautie brighte,
Entice you efte with vayne delighte.

And Lullaby my wanton will,
Lette reasons rule, nowe reigne thy thought,
Since all to late I finde my skyll,
Howe deare I have thy fansies bought :
With Lullaby nowe tak thyne ease,
With Lullaby thy doubtes appease :
For trust to this, if thou be styll,
My body shall obey thy will.

Thus Lullabye my youth, myne eyes,
My will, my ware, and all that was,
I can no mo delayes devise,
But welcome payne, let pleasure passe :
With Lullaby now take your leave,
With Lullaby your dreames deceive,
And when you rise with waking eye,
Remember then this Lullabye.

George Turberville, a west-country gentleman born
about 1640, wrote well for his age, and once at least
well for any :

The greene that you did wish mee weare
　　Aye for your loove,
And on my helme a braunch to beare,
　　Not to remoove :
Was ever you to have in minde,
Whom Cupid hath my Feere assignde.

As I in this have done your will,
　　And minde to doo :

So I request you to fulfill
　　My fansie too :
A greene and loving heart to have,
And this is all that I doe crave.

For if your flowring heart should chaunge
　　His colour greene.
Or you at length a Ladie straunge
　　Of mee be seene :
Then will my braunch against his use
His colour chaunge for your refuse.

As Winters force can not deface
　　This braunch his hue :
So let no chaunge of love disgrace
　　Your friendship true :
You were mine owne and so be still,
So shall we live and love our fill

Then may I thinke my selfe to bee
　　Well recompenst,
For wearing of the Tree that is
　　So well defenst
Agaynst all weather that doth fall,
When waywarde Winter spits his gall.

And when wee meete, to trie me true,
　　Looke on my hed,
And I will crave an oth of you
　　Where Faith be fled :
So shall we both assured bee,
Both I of you, and you of mee.

We may pause for an instant with John Still, Bishop
of Bath and Wells, born about the same time, who may
have been the author of *Gammer Gurton's Needle*, the

second English comedy to be written. The prelate could turn as good a drinking song as any one of his time :

> Back and side go bare ! go bare !
> Both foot and hand go cold !
> But belly, God send thee good ale enough ;
> Whether it be new or old !

I cannot eat but little meat ; my stomach is not good ;
But, sure, I think that I can drink with him that wears a hood !
Though I go bare ; take ye no care, I am nothing acold !
I stuff my skin so full within of jolly good ale and old.
>   Back and side go bare ! go bare ! &c.

I love no roast but a nut-brown toast, and a crab laid in the
>   fire !
A little bread shall do me stead ! much bread I not desire !
No frost, nor snow, no wind, I trow, can hurt me if I would ;
I am so wrapped, and thoroughly lapped of jolly good ale
>   and old !
>   Back and side go bare ! go bare ! &c.

Thomas Sackville, Earl of Dorset, born some ten years later than Gascoigne, is a poet who has been enthusiastically praised by many of the best critics. It is true that his *Induction* has a musical solemnity of movement that no one else in his time could match, and that alone is enough to warrant eulogy.

> Thence come we to the horrour and the hell,
> The large great kingdoms, and the dreadful reign
> Of Pluto in his throne where he did dwell,
> The wide waste places, and the hugy plain,
> The wailings, shrieks, and sundry sorts of pain,
> The sighs, the sobs, the deep and deadly groan :
> Earth, air, and all, resounding plaint and moan.

Here pul'd the babes, and here the maids unwed
With folded hands their sorry chance bewail'd,
Here wept the guiltless slain, and lovers dead,
That slew themselves when nothing else avail'd :
A thousand sorts of sorrows here, that wail'd
With sighs, and tears, sobs, shrieks, and all yfear,
That, oh, alas, it was a hell to hear.

Yes, that is good by any standard, though when we
look forward from it to the long future of poetry in
England, we feel, unhandsomely perhaps, that it has
rather the merit of being the first in a manner than
the best. But that a poet has possibly been allowed a
little more than his due is no reason for allowing him
a little less. Sackville, who wrote his poetry in the
intervals of diplomacy, was a good poet at a time when
they were still rare. If it comes to that, they have
never been anything else. Of the countless millions
of Englishmen who have lived, perhaps two hundred
at a guess have been good poets. One fine line of
verse is a miracle against all the tables of mortality.
But, looking at poetry in its own narrow confines,
Sackville was a poet in an age when poets were
rare, and he wrote on the threshold of an age when
they were not. He and Gascoigne are worth a pil-
grimage.

Sir Philip Sidney, who, like most of his illustrious
contemporaries, inherited family memories of the Tudor
partiality for bloody scenes on Tower Hill, has become
a legendary figure known to every school-child. He
was the friend and idol of a literary group which in-
cluded Fulke Greville, Edward Dyer, Edmund Spenser
and, more distantly, Gabriel Harvey, who seduced them
for a time to share his own delusion that English verse

ought to be reformed by the introduction of classical prosody. Fortunately the fit was a short one, and left no bad after-effects. Dyer achieved a peak of immortality with one line—

My mind to me a Kingdom is,

and Fulke Greville, who dying after a crowded and distinguished life at the age of seventy-four was content to have recorded on his grave the single fact that he had been Philip Sidney's friend, is honoured rather in his friendship and his character than his poetry. We can admire his verse without remembering it. But his name will always be one of gracious associations. Sidney himself wrote a sequence of sonnets, *Astrophel and Stella*, some of which have become deservedly famous, among them

With how sad steps, O Moon, thou climb'st the skies !
How silently, and with how wan a face !
What, may it be that even in heavenly place
That busy archer his sharp arrows tries !
Sure, if that long-with-love-acquainted eyes
Can judge of love, thou feel'st a lover's case,
I read it in thy looks ; thy languisht grace,
To me, that feel the like, thy state descries.
Then, even of fellowship, O Moon, tell me,
Is constant love deem'd there but want of wit ?
Are beauties there as proud as here they be ?
Do they above love to be lov'd, and yet
Those lovers scorn whom that love doth possess ?
Do they call virtue there ungratefulness ?

His best poem otherwise is the *Dirge*, with its striking anticipation of Swinburne's *Garden of Proserpine* :

Ring out your bells, let mourning shews be spread ;
For Love is dead :
  All Love is dead, infected
With plague of deep disdain :
  Worth, as nought worth, rejected,
And Faith fair scorn doth gain.
  From so ungrateful fancy,
  From such a female frenzy,
  From them that use men thus,
  Good Lord, deliver us !

Weep, neighbours, weep ; do you not hear it said
That Love is dead ?
  His death-bed, peacock's folly ;
His winding-sheet is shame ;
  His will, false-seeming wholly ;
His sole executor, blame.
  From so ungrateful fancy,
  From such a female frenzy,
  From them that use men thus,
  Good Lord, deliver us !

Let dirge be sung, and trentals rightly read,
For Love is dead ;
  Sir Wrong his tomb ordaineth
My mistress' marble heart ;
  Which epitaph containeth,
'Her eyes were once his dart.'
  From so ungrateful fancy,
  From such a female frenzy,
  From them that use men thus,
  Good Lord, deliver us !

Alas, I lie : rage hath this error bred :
Love is not dead ;
  Love is not dead, but sleepeth
In her unmatchèd mind,
  Where she his counsel keepeth,

9

Till due deserts she find.
  Therefore from so vile fancy,
  To call such wit a frenzy,
  Who Love can temper thus,
  Good Lord, deliver us !

When Sidney died in 1586, Spenser lamented his loss
in a series of elegies that are among his own best lyric
verse.   Dedicating *The Ruines of Time* to Mary Countess
of Pembroke, Sidney's sister, he speaks of ' that most
noble spirit, which was the hope of all learned men,
and the patron of my young Muses'.   These stanzas,
from *An Elegie, or Friend's Passion, for His Astrophill*,
show at once the force of Spenser's grief, and the arrival
of English verse at its golden age :

When he descended down the mount,
His personage seemed most divine,
A thousand graces one might count,
Upon his lovely cheerfull eine ;
  To heare him speake and sweetly smile,
  You were in Paradise the while.

A sweet attractive kinde of grace,
A full assurance given by lookes,
Continuall comfort in a face,
The lineaments of gospell bookes,
  I trowe that countenance cannot lie,
  Whose thoughts are legible in the eie.

Was never eie did see that face
Was never eare did heare that tong,
Was never minde did minde his grace,
That ever thought the travell long ;
  But eies and eares, and ev'ry thought,
  Were with his sweete perfections caught.

O God, that such a worthy man,
In whom so rare desarts did raigne,
Desired thus, must leave us than,
And we to wish for him in vaine !
  O could the stars, that bred that wit,
  In force no longer fixed sit !

Here was an authority that had not been heard since
Chaucer, and it had now drawn lyric into its scope.
Spenser's lyric achievement, indeed, was immeasurably
above anything of the sort that had been done before
him. *Amoretti* as a sonnet sequence is as good as any
but Shakespeare's, though far from being as good as
his. *The Shephearde's Calendar*, designed on a large
scale of lyric pastoral, is, like some women, more lovely
than interesting. But in the *Epithalamion*, the *Prothal-
amion* and *The Four Hymns* addressed respectively to
Love, Beauty, Heavenly Love, and Heavenly Beauty,
Spenser, who seldom attempted the shorter—though
certainly not less difficult—flight of the song, attempted
an ampler lyric architecture, and for comparable success
we have to look to things on the scale of *Lycidas* and
the *Ode on the Intimations of Immortality* and *Adonais*, and
the *Ode to a Nightingale*. Spenser's great lyric poems
may not reach the perfection of these, but they are in this
class, and they cannot be measured by any other standard.
This from the *Hymn* to Beauty is, while missing the
shape of the whole, an indication of its quality.

How vainely then doe ydle wits inuent,
That beautie is nought else, but mixture made
Of colours faire, and goodly temp'rament
Of pure complexions, that shall quickly fade
And passe away, like to a sommers shade,
Or that it is but comely composition
Of parts well measurd, with meet disposition.

Hath white and red in it such wondrous powre,
That it can pierce through th'eyes vnto the hart,
And therein stirre such rage and restless stowre,
As nought but death can stint his dolours smart?
Or can proportion of the outward part,
Moue such affection in the inward mynd,
That it can rob both sense and reason blynd?

Why doe not then the blossomes of the field,
Which are arayd with much more orient hew,
And to the sense most daintie odours yield,
Worke like impression in the lookers vew?
Or why doe not faire pictures like powre shew,
In which oftimes, we Nature see of Art
Exceld, in perfect limming euery part.

But ah, beleeue me, there is more than so
That workes such wonders in the minds of men.
I that have often prou'd, too well it know;
And who so list the like assayes to ken,
Shall find by tryall, and confesse it then,
That Beautie is not, as fond men misdeeme,
An outward shew of things, that onely seeme.

For that same goodly hew of white and red,
With which the cheekes are sprinckled, shall decay,
And those sweete rosy leaues so fairely spred
Vpon the lips, shall fade and fall away
To that they were, euen to corrupted clay.
That golden wyre, those sparckling stars so bright
Shall turne to dust, and loose their goodly light.

But that faire lampe, from whose celestiall ray
That light proceedes, which kindleth louers fire,
Shall neuer be extinguisht nor decay,

But when the vitall spirits doe expyre,
Vnto her natiue planet shall retyre,
For it is heauenly borne and can not die,
Being a parcell if the purest skie.

Saintsbury—needless to say, in full recognition of their excellence—declared that these major lyrics were nevertheless 'but the chapels and chantries of the *Fäerie Queen*'. It may be so, but, splendid as the cathedral is, some of us may find ourselves in it less often than in the chapels and chantries.

With the establishment of Spenser, we are approaching the full song of the Elizabethans of Shakespeare's age. There was but a twelve-year difference between the ages of the two poets, but they were twelve years of quite disproportionate historical significance. Nearly contemporary though he was, Spenser as a poet belonged to an earlier epoch than Shakespeare. His work, abounding in new assurance and authority, still shows traces everywhere of the long experimental generations between Chaucer and himself. In Shakespeare they are almost wholly absent. Spenser was the bridge between a long age of poetic trial and error and a relatively brief age of perfectly though not over-matured accomplishment, an age of great poets that has fittingly taken its name from one. There is one poem, anonymous and of uncertain date, which not improbably belongs to this transitional period. It is the loveliest religious lyric before the seventeenth century, and one of the loveliest in the language. It shall, with one other, lead us from Spenser to the later Elizabethans.

PREPARATIONS

Yet if His Majesty, our sovereign lord,
Should of his own accord
Friendly himself invite,
And say 'I'll be your guest to-morrow night',
How should we stir ourselves, call and command
All hands to work ! 'Let no man idle stand.'

'Set me fine Spanish tables in the hall ;
See they be fitted all ;
Let there be room to eat
And order taken that there want no meat.
See every sconce and candlestick made bright,
That without tapers they may give a light.

'Look to the presence : are the carpets spread,
The dazie o'er the head,
The cushions in the chairs,
And all the candles lighted on the stairs ?
Perfume the chambers, and in any case
Let each man give attendance in his place !'

Thus, if a king were coming, would we do ;
And 'twere good reason too ;
For 'tis a duteous thing
To show all honour to an earthly king,
And after all our travail and our cost,
So he be pleased, to think no labour lost.

But at the coming of the King of Heaven
All's set at six and seven ;
We wallow in our sin,
Christ cannot find a chamber in the inn.
We entertain Him always like a stranger,
And, as at first, still lodge Him in the manger.

The other is *The Burning Babe*, worthy to stand by it, and as fine as anything ever written in English ' four-teeners'. It is by Robert Southwell, a young Jesuit priest who was executed at Tyburn in 1594 at the age of thirty-two, another example of the civilizing influence of church brawls in history :

As I in hoary winter's night stood shivering in the snow,
Surprised I was with sudden heat which made my heart to
  glow ;
And lifting up a fearful eye to view what fire was near,
A pretty babe all burning bright did in the air appear,
Who scorched with exceeding heat such floods of tears did
  shed,
As though His floods should quench His flames with what
  His tears were fed ;
Alas ! quoth He, but newly born in fiery hearts of fry,
Yet none approach to warm their hearts or feel my fire but I !
My faultless breast the furnace is, the fuel wounding thorns ;
Love is the fire and sighs the smoke, the ashes shame and
  scorns ;
The fuel Justice layeth on, and Mercy blows the coals ;
The metal in this furnace wrought are men's defiled souls ;
For which, as now on fire I am, to work them to their good,
So will I melt into a bath, to wash them in my blood :
With this He vanish'd out of sight, and swiftly shrunk away,
And straight I called unto mind that it was Christmas-day.

IX

ELIZABETHAN LYRIC

THE LOVE POETRY

LYRIC was one of the two main activities in Elizabethan poetry, the other being drama. Many of the chief poets wrote both with equal mastery. If the lyric production of the age has on the whole to be of less commanding importance than the drama, it is less only than that. Lacking it, English poetry would lack one of its brightest honours.

It would be an exaggeration to say that the sole theme of the Elizabethan lyric was love ; but it is certainly true that if we took the love poetry away from the reckoning, a few pieces on mortality and a few—very few—nature lyrics are about all of any consequence that would be left. Love, in fact, though not quite the exclusive lyric theme, was incomparably the most general. The great sonnet sequences, which together account for a considerable proportion of the age's lyric poetry, are concerned virtually with nothing else, and the same is true of nine songs out of ten. As a presiding influence on lyric poetry love was unchallenged, and the circumstance is one of far-reaching significance, as we shall see.

From time to time critics have been at pains to show, largely by the citation of parallel passages, that the

124

Elizabethan love poems were mostly no more than poetical exercises by gifted young men intoxicated by draughts, more or less shallow, of renascence culture. In recent times Sir Sidney Lee, to whose scholarship we all owe so much, was the most eminent and the most confident of these. To find the French or Italian source of an English love poem was enough to convince him that love had very little to do with it. Even if it had to be admitted that the original was genuinely inspired by passion, the English poet was allowed no credit on that account. Love, in other words, was not a profound but a fashionable emotion, and if you had the trick of writing, you could learn from the example of continental poets how to establish an agreeable literary reputation for gallantry. That is, I think, not an over-statement of a view that has not infrequently been advanced by otherwise responsible critics. It is a view unsupported by any semblance of reality.

It is true that the Elizabethan love poets borrowed conventions and imagery from foreign masters, and that there were certain standards of amorous technique or deportment of which they all took some notice. These standards cover a wide range of despair, doubt, servility, defiance, satisfaction ; but there is a kinship between all the figures. It is true also that in most of this love poetry it is useless to look for biographical disclosures. But all this lends no colour to the absurd notion that the poetry itself is inspired by an intellectual conceit and not by the heart's fire. Many years ago, when I was quite a young man, I discussed this question in the introduction to an edition of Philip Sidney's poems. My view had the good fortune to be supported by John Bailey, who made his own statement of it in words that are conclusive :

This is the poetry which Mr. Drinkwater makes more accessible by his handy little volume. He prefaces it with two introductions, a biographical and a critical ; both competently and sensibly done, telling the plain reader all he need know about the man and the poet. On the thorny and controversial question of the relation in which the poet's sonnets stand to the facts of his life, the relation of Astrophel and Stella to Philip Sidney and Penelope Devereux, he takes, if we may dare to brave some distinguished critics enough to say so, the only line that is possible to a man who knows what poetry is. Dante and Beatrice, Petrarch and Laura, Sidney and Stella, Shelley and Emilia Viviani, Shakespeare and the mysterious youth—these are not fictions, still less are they facts. They are poetry, which is neither fiction nor fact but truth. To suppose that the convincing intensity of the *Vita Nuova* or the sonnets of Sidney or Shakespeare proves that they are newspaper biographies of their subjects is simply to show that the critic does not understand the nature of poetry. To suppose that the slightness, coldness, and bareness of the relations of the lovers in actual fact, so far as we know them, prove that the poems are mere fictions, is simply to make the same mistake from the opposite side. Great poets do not live in a vacuum ; they have their eyes and hands on life, their own life and the lives of others. The poet finds in life the stuff of his work ; but he never leaves it as he finds it. He touches nothing without transfiguring it, recreating it, giving it new birth ; and only one who should have as great a genius for seeing prose in poetry as the poet has for seeing poetry in prose could rediscover the facts out of a reading of the poems. Sidney was in love ' with an ideal of his own ', as Mr. Drinkwater says.

The Elizabethan age was one of intense national vitality, which was reflected in its poetry. The poets were vehemently alive with the discovery, the adventure, the expansion of their time. Miranda's ' brave new world ' was building before their eyes, and they took eager delight in it. It was a young, positive age, without misgivings or reservations, and the mood of poetry was tuned to the same pitch. Elizabeth was often a tiresome and dangerous woman, but on the throne of Gloriana's court she took the imagination of every one in the country, poets and all.

In other words, the poets were acutely sensitive to the teeming life of England, its germinating commerce and travel, philosophy and science, war and courtly enterprise. And, in their lyrics, they sang of love and of little else. It is a deeply significant fact. How often are we told that it is the poet's business to particularize the life of his day in his poetry ? The brief demand is that he should be ' modern ', in the sense, we are given to understand, that Mr. T. S. Eliot, for example, is modern while Mr. de la Mare, for example, is not. I have no intention of noticing the critical affectations that have done much to bring even the better poetry since the so-called Georgians into ridicule, but this question of ' modernity ' requires a word. Mr. Eliot is a poet of distinction, one of several in our time, and it is not his fault that he has been misrepresented as above his by no means inconsiderable stature by un-informed and imperceptive judgements. Nor can he find much pleasure in being praised for qualities that are not notably laudable. Most conspicuous of these is this modernity. An image much admired by his less securely balanced admirers is :

> Let us go then, you and I,
> When the evening is spread out against the sky
> Like a patient etherized upon a table.

Thus, we are told, is the modern vision vindicated, and the poet justified of his calling. But what simple-minded nonsense is this. The image of the evening as an etherized patient is not inappropriate ; it is even striking, and the word ' etherized ' has an adroit beauty in its place. But if the image is modern, is it not also upstart and fugitive ? What will have become of it two hundred years hence when its novelty has gone and its meaning has probably long been out of date ? When Words-worth said that the evening was breathless with adora-tion as a Nun, he was using an image that was not novel (although it was original) and would never tarnish ; when Mr. Eliot says that the evening is like an etherized patient on an operating-table he uses an image that is novel and will perish. It may well be that he sets no great store by it himself, but it is the sort of thing that we are called upon most to admire in him, which is foolish.

The Elizabethan lyrists sang of love, and they sang of it in terms that Chaucer might have used, to tunes of their later but not strange invention. That is to say, in a world excitingly crowded with new interest and event, to which their senses were alert, they sang of a fundamental passion, indifferent to novelty. Shake-speare asks the direct question :

> Why is my verse so barren of new pride ?
> So far from variation or quick change ?
> Why, with the time, do I not glance aside
> To new-found methods and to compounds strange ?
> Why write I still all one, ever the same,
> And keep invention in a noted weed . . . ?

and the answer is that, writing of his love, which like the sun is daily new and old, 'all his best is dressing old words new '. I said just now that ' the Elizabethan age was one of intense national vitality, which was

reflected in its poetry'. That is true of its lyric poetry
no less than of its dramatic. But it is precisely the
vitality that is reflected, not the circumstance or ' modern-
ity '. Lovers at any time might have written these
poems, granted the gift to write them. Shakespeare's
reference to ' new-found methods ' and ' compounds
strange ' touches on long-forgotten eccentricities of
which we do not even know the nature. He and his
fellows, the magnificently original and impenitently
traditional poets of their time, wrote poetry not a note
or, merely linguistic considerations apart, a phrase of
which would have been out of place in Chaucer or
would be out of place in the poet whose poems are not
yet written. And any view of poetry which fails to
recognize the significance of this can be but a very
imperfect one.

After the Elizabethans, love was to remain, as it
always must, a principal motive in lyric poetry, but
other themes, nature most successfully, were to rival its
supremacy. Of the Elizabethan love poems many of
the best, fortunately, are also the best known, and such
things as Marlowe's ' Come live with me and be my
love ', and Ben Jonson's ' Drink to me only with thine
eyes ', and Henry Wotton's ' You meaner beauties of
the night ', and any dozen of Shakespeare's songs and
sonnets, are almost too familiar for quotation, though
quoted some of them must be. But less celebrated things
are hardly less representative. Even quite unconsidered
poets like Joshua Sylvester, the monumental translator
of Du Bartas, could once in a while rise to—

> Were I as base as is the lowly plain,
> And you, my Love, as high as heaven above,

thereby glancing a little reproachfully at so sure a critic

as Saintsbury for saying that he had ' neither cry nor
song in him '.   In the lighter, but not therefore irrespon-
sible kind of conceit, nothing could be more charm-
ing than this song by Thomas Campion, a musical
physician :

> There is a garden in her face
>   Where roses and white lilies blow ;
> A heavenly paradise is that place,
>   Wherein all pleasant fruits do flow :
>   Where cherries grow which none may buy
>   Till ' Cherry-ripe ' themselves do cry.
>
> Those cherries fairly do enclose
>   Of orient pearl a double row,
> Which when her lovely laughter shows,
>   They look like rose-buds fill'd with snow ;
>   Yet them nor peer nor prince can buy
>   Till ' Cherry-ripe ' themselves do cry.
>
> Her eyes like angels watch them still ;
>   Her brows like bended bows do stand,
> Threat'ning with piercing frowns to kill
>   All that attempt with eye or hand
>   Those sacred cherries to come nigh,
>   Till ' Cherry-ripe ' themselves do cry.

Although not strictly a love poem, it is so much of a
mood with the love poetry of the time, and so graciously
contrived, that I must find a place here for Richard
Barnfield's sonnet :

> If music and sweet poetry agree,
> As they must needs, the sister and the brother,
> Then must the love be great 'twixt thee and me,
> Because thou lov'st the one, and I the other.

Dowland to thee is dear, whose heavenly touch
Upon the lute doth ravish human sense ;
Spenser to me, whose deep conceit is such
As, passing all conceit, needs no defence.
Thou lov'st to hear the sweet melodious sound
That Phoebus' lute, the queen of music, makes ;
And I in deep delight am chiefly drown'd
Whenas himself to singing he betakes.
   One god is god of both, as poets feign ;
   One knight loves both, and both in thee remain.

Then there was the unfortunate Robert Greene, four
years older than Marvell but dead before him, who
spent much of his short life in fussy literary feuds, with
Shakespeare as one of his animosities, and yet could find
moods for such heavenly jingle as :

   Sweet Adon ! dar'st not glance thine eye
     N'oserez vous, mon bel ami !
   Upon thy Venus, that must die !
    Je vous en prie, pity me !
     N'oserez vous, mon bel ! mon bel !
     N'oserez vous, mon bel ami !

   See, how sad thy Venus lies,
     N'oserez vous, mon bel ami !
   Love in heart, and tears in eyes !
    Je vous en prie, pity me !
     N'oserez vous, mon bel ! mon bel !
     N'oserez vous, mon bel ami !

   Thy face as fair as Paphos' brooks ;
     N'oserez vous, mon bel ami !
   Wherein Fancy baits her hooks.
    Je vous en prie, pity me !
     N'oserez vous, mon bel ! mon bel !
     N'oserez vous, mon bel ami !

Thy cheeks like cherries that do grow
N'oserez vous, mon bel ami !
Amongst the western mounts of snow.
Je vous en prie, pity me !
  N'oserez vous, mon bel ! mon bel !
  N'oserez vous, mon bel ami !

Thy lips vermilion, full of love,
N'oserez vous, mon bel ami !
Thy neck as silver, white as dove.
Je vous en prie, pity me !
  N'oserez vous, mon bel ! mon bel !
  N'oserez vous, mon bel ami !

Thine eyes, like flames of holy fires,
N'oserez vous, mon bel ami !
Burn all my thoughts, with sweet desires !
Je vous en prie, pity me !
  N'oserez vous, mon bel ! mon bel !
  N'oserez vous, mon bel ami !

All thy beauties sting my heart !
N'oserez vous, mon bel ami !
I must die, through Cupid's dart !
Je vous en prie, pity me !
  N'oserez vous, mon bel ! mon bel !
  N'oserez vous, mon bel ami !

Wilt thou let thy Venus die ?
N'oserez vous, mon bel ami !
Adon. were unkind ! say I !
Je vous en prie, pity me !
  N'oserez vous, mon bel ! mon bel !
  N'oserez vous, mon bel ami !

To let fair Venus die for woe !
N'oserez vous, mon bel ami !
That doth sweet Adon. so !
Je vous en prie, pity me !
N'oserez vous, mon bel ! mon bel !
N'oserez vous, mon bel ami !

Nicholas Breton, who, born in 1545, performed the
very unusual feat for that age of living to be over eighty,
could make so good a beginning as :

On a hill there grows a flower,
Fair befall the dainty sweet !
By that flower, there is a bower ;
Where the heavenly Muses meet.

In that bower, there is a chair,
Fringèd all about with gold ;
Where doth sit the fairest Fair
That ever eye did yet behold,

but somehow never managed to keep it up throughout
even a short poem. Of Thomas Lodge, too, whose
Rosalynde gave Shakespeare material for *As You Like It*,
three verses are usually better than five :

My Phillis hath the morning sun
At first to look upon her ;
And Phillis hath morn-waking birds,
Her risings for to honour.

My Phillis hath prime-feathered flowers,
That smile when she treads on them ;
And Phillis hath a gallant flock,
That leap, since she doth own them.

But Phillis hath so hard a heart,
  Alas, that she should have it !
As yields no mercy to desert,
  Nor grace to those that crave it.

Lodge was born in 1558, George Wither thirty years later. The perfect example of the defiant lyric to set beside such things as Lodge's lament is the younger poet's *Resolution*, which although in date it belongs to the Jacobean and not the Elizabethan age, is still of the age that Shakespeare knew and made :

Shall I, wasting in despaire
Dye, because a woman's fair ?
Or make pale my cheeks with care
Cause anothers Rosie are ?
  Be she fairer than the Day
  Or the flowry Meads in May,
  If she thinke not well of me,
  What care I *how* faire she be ?

Shall my seely heart be pin'd
Cause I see a woman kind ?
Or a well disposed Nature
Joyned with a lovely feature ?
  Be she Meeker, Kinder than
  Turtle-dove or *Pellican :*
  If she be not so to me,
  What care I how kind she be ?

Shall a woman's Vertues move
Me to perish for her Love ?
Or her wel deservings knowne
Make me quite forget mine own ?
  Be she with that Goodness blest
  Which may merit name of best :
  If she be not such to me,
  What care I how Good she be ?

Cause her *Fortune* seems too high
Shall I play the fool and die ?
She that beares a Noble mind,
If not outward helpes she find,
   Thinks what with them he wold do,
   That without them dares her woe.
And unlesse that *Minde* I see,
What care I how great she be ?

Great, or Good, or Kind, or Faire
I will ne'er the more despaire :
If she love me (this beleeve)
I will Die ere she shall grieve.
   If she slight me when I woe,
   I can scorne and let her goe,
For if she be not for me,
What care I for whom she be ?

The use of the term ' Elizabethan ' to designate this great age of English lyric is in fact questionable, since much of the finest work was done after Elizabeth's death, when the first splendid impulse of national renascence was waning. Shakespeare himself, the very fugleman of Elizabethan poetry, wrote much of his greatest work under James, and although drama was then—so far as we know—his only concern, *Cymbeline* and *The Tempest* provide sufficient evidence that his lyric powers had not declined even from the sonnets. If we call it ' the Shakespearean age ', then, we are on safer ground, and with George Wither we pass to some of its later poets and their love songs.

In the pursuit of our own concerns, in our occupations, we are, and mercifully, seldom able or tempted to confront ourselves with the old insoluble enigmas. It is a very disconcerting, but fortunately rare experience, with some letters to post, three appointments to keep, a publisher's demands to be satisfied, and the housekeeping books next Friday to be settled, suddenly to pull up in Baker Street and say, ' What am I ? Where do I come from ? What is to be the end of it all ? I do not know. I know just nothing at all about it.' Similarly, in philosophy and aesthetics, there are insurmountable and impenetrable barriers against thought. What *is* life ? The scientists are noble, heroic, in their investigations, and at last they can tell us no more than the chimney-sweeper. What is good, and what evil ? The philosophers, assuming serene detachment, have nevertheless wrangled about it since the mind of man made its first nebulous efforts to organize itself. What, in turn, is beauty ? Why do I find Ver Meer's painting of Delft inexpressibly lovely, and Charing Cross Bridge inexpressibly hideous ? Cudgel my mind as I will, I still arrive at no satisfactory intellectual explanation of a fact that is as clear to my consciousness as that I need food when I am hungry. And if some bold aesthetician should seek a simple test for an inquiry into this radical problem of our existence, he might do far worse than choose to ask—why is the sonnet a form of such impressive and durable delight in English poetry ? Why, for instance, has it been decided beyond appeal that fourteen lines are righter than sixteen or twelve ? Why should those fourteen inexorably be split into eight and six ? Why should it be necessary in the nature of things for it to be rhymed and not blank ? Why should the statement of the first part exist only in the application of the second ? Why should its line require five feet rather than four or six ? Why should its rhyming scheme allow alternation but not couplet sequences ? To answer these questions by saying that so, and so alone is the effect achieved, is no more than the child's answer to the question, ' Why don't you want to go for a walk this morning ? '—' Because I don't.'

In the Elizabethan love poetry the sonnet was the major, the most authoritative form. Whenever the emotion rose to the finer heights of passion, fourteen lines, distributed to one of two or three prescribed patterns, took command of the poet's invention. We must, after all, call Shakespeare in evidence :

> When to the sessions of sweet silent thought
> I summon up remembrance of things past,
> I sigh the lack of many a thing I sought,
> And with old woes new wail my dear time's waste :
> Then can I drown an eye, unus'd to flow,
> For precious friends hid in death's dateless night,
> And weep afresh love's long since cancell'd woe,
> And moan the expense of many a vanish'd sight :
> Then can I grieve at grievances foregone,
> And heavily from woe to woe tell o'er
> The sad account of fore-bemoaned moan,
> Which I new pay, as if not paid before.
>   But if the while I think on thee, dear friend,
>   All losses are restor'd, and sorrows end.

That is the final speech, in its final shape. Human invention cannot rise above it. Why ? The answer will still evade us, but, for want of better idleness, let us attempt it.

One of the most astonishing things ever said by a great poet about the art of poetry is to be found in Milton's note on the verse of *Paradise Lost*.

The measure is *English* Heroic Verse without Rime, as that of *Homer* in *Greek*, and of *Virgil* in *Latin* ; Rime being no necessary Adjunct or true Ornament of Poem or good

Verse, in longer Works especially, but the Invention of a barbarous Age, to set off wretched matter and lame Meeter ; grac't indeed since by the use of some famous modern Poets, carried away by Custom, but much to thir own vexation, hindrance, and constraint to express many things otherwise, and for the most part worse then else they would have exprest them. Not without cause therefore some both *Italian* and *Spanish* Poets of prime note have rejected Rime both in longer and shorter Works, as have also long since our best *English* Tragedies, as a thing of it self, to all judicious eares, triveal and of no true musical delight ; which consists only in apt Numbers, fit quantity of Syllables, and the sense variously drawn out from one Verse into another, not in the jingling sound of like endings, a fault avoyded by the learned Ancients both in Poetry and all good Oratory. This neglect then of Rime so little is to be taken for a defect, though it may seem so perhaps to vulgar Readers, that it rather is to be esteem'd an example set, the first in *English*, of ancient liberty recover'd to Heroic Poem from the trouble-som and modern bondage of Rimeing.

Milton was always headstrong in debate, and when he had a cause to plead was readily, too readily excited. He was now pleading the cause of blank verse, having decided on that measure for the great work to which he had given so many years of preparation. But there was not the smallest need for him to get so heated about it. No one was likely to quarrel with him for the use of an instrument that, as he himself said, had long since been established in English poetry by the highest example. It is true that when he was writing it was not a fashionable form with the poets, but he could very well have afforded to neglect any irresponsible censure that his choice might have provoked. But that was not Milton's dialectical way. When he scented controversy, he was all for getting the first word in. He got it in here, with quite inappropriate emphasis. Nobody in his senses could then or at any time have wished *Paradise Lost* to be in rhyme, but the majestic triumph of Milton's blank verse in his ' Heroic Poem ' obviously does nothing to leave rhyme discredited. His little diatribe against this ' triveal ' thing, ' of no musical delight ', comes oddly from the poet of *Lycidas*, but Milton in prose argument, although he could be over- whelming, was frequently irrational. Such talk about rhyme is, in fact, rubbish, as he himself would have been ready to prove on any other occasion.

It is true that weak versifiers are often constrained by the necessities of rhyme to ' express many things other- wise, and for the most part worse than else they would have exprest them ', but it is in any case of small con- sequence what incompetence expresses or fails to express. It is true also that rhyme is ' no necessary Adjunct . . . of Poem or good Verse ', so obviously true, indeed, as to be hardly worth saying. Further, it is true that rhyme is no ' necessary . . . Ornament of Poem or good Verse ', but not true in the sense that Milton intends. For rhyme, when rightly employed, as it has been by countless poems from Chaucer down to the present time, is no mere ornament of verse, but an organic element of it. Finally, the assertion that rhyme in the practice of good Verse, in *Lycidas*, for example, is used ' to set off wretched matter and lame Meeter ', is so silly as to make it seem impossible that Milton could have been serious when he wrote it. Since, however, if Milton was ever unserious in any way it certainly was not in that way, we can only say that he was, not for the first time, wrong-headed, and leave it at that.

Rhyme is an organic element of the verse in which it is fitly employed. It affords us a deeper satisfaction

than we can ever derive from applied ornament, which,
however elegant or gracious it may be, is something
essentially inorganic to the structure that it adorns.
The satisfaction of rhyme is the satisfaction of measurable
expectancy fulfilled, which is one of the cardinal delights
of the mind.   Why this is a cardinal delight, and why
the expectancy of rhyming sound should be pleasurable,
are questions which bring us near to that region of
experience where reason is no longer sure of itself.   But,
although we may not be able to explain why these
things are, we can a little further elaborate our definition
of what they are.

The delight of fulfilled expectancy is but a minor
variation on the larger delight that proceeds from all
art, or, in wider terms, of all creation.   The evocation
of cosmos out of chaos, of shape out of flux, of the
comprehensible out of the incomprehensible, this is the
supreme satisfaction of the human and, so far as we can
surmise, of the divine mind.   As we succeed in this,
so do we approach the heights of happy wisdom ;   as
we fail, so do we sink towards the abyss of insanity.
The last desire of Milton's Penseroso is to 'rightly spell'
the world,

> Till old experience do attain
> To something like prophetic strain.

Experience translated into prophecy :   there is the true
vision of content, turned to a commonsense note by
Byron, 'the best of Prophets of the Future is the Past'.
The American Patrick Henry had said it in even plainer
prose fifty years before Byron, 'I know of no way of
judging of the future but by the past'.   It's all one.
The employment of experience to revelation of what
is to come, the quiet assurance that given conditions

come to given effects, realized in such sober certainties
as that as the day sets to-night it will break to-morrow,
or in the fortitude that knows all grief to have an
ending, these are the circumstances that lie at the roots
of all victorious life. Which takes a step at least further
towards discovery of the delight that is in fulfilled
expectancy.

I made the qualification above that the expectancy
should itself be pleasurable. I need not go beyond
that here to examine whether even expectancy that is
not obviously or demonstrably pleasurable is or is not
delightful in fulfilment, though in the long view of
human experience it probably is. For the present pur-
pose it is enough to claim that when the expectancy is
pleasurable, the fulfilment is at the height of human
satisfaction. And rhyme, in a confined but representa-
tive way, is such a fulfilment.

The conveyance of meaning by language is a matter
of the greatest complexity. The life of a word is
organically comprised of many elements. Let us take
a word that is not of major significance, as are such
words as life and death, love and mind and peace ;
let us take the word ' rhyme ' itself, for example.

As we spell it out, r-h-y-m-e, we make for ourselves
a symbol that is intellectually recognized by common
consent. The word thus is as concrete in substance as
a flag- or a kerb-stone, finding its place in the dictionary
to denote ' the recurrence of similar sounds at certain
intervals ,'. But the word has sound as well as sense.
For some reason it sounds like the thing it is. When
Shakespeare writes of ' beauty, making beautiful old
rhyme ', we know on the instant that his appeal is to
a vital assonance in experience, and we know it rather
by the sound of the word than by its literal sense. We

have, then, the concrete or substantial form of the word, and the other, perhaps larger instruction of sound. Then, beyond these again, we have a significance that reaches into the far origins of language. 'Rhyme', as Shakespeare here uses the word, is both concrete and aural in value, but it is also associative. And here, I think, we come upon the obscurest but nevertheless the profoundest secret of rhyme as a figure in poetry. In the evolution of language as used by the masters, words have fallen into groups in which wide extremes have been brought into fundamental correspondence. For this, as for most of the larger interpretations of life, the poets are chiefly responsible. 'Death—breath', 'cease—peace', 'rest—best', 'earth—birth', 'lost—cost', 'heart—part', 'blind—mind', 'went—spent', 'hate—fate', 'womb—tomb', 'sear—fear', 'wail—pale', 'weep—deep', 'seems—dreams', 'spirit—inherit', 'youth—truth'—why are these and an infinity of other rhyming couples found, through six centuries of English poetry, in endlessly well-matched union? It cannot be attributed to accident. Nor will any law of averages account for it. There is only one explanation, which is that in the evolution of experience to the mould of words, the mind of man has been constantly inspired to an alchemic subtlety of associative sound.

And so, when Shakespeare ends the line of a sonnet with the word 'rhyme', we expect an answer to the sound which is not only assonant but also associative. If we light upon the line by chance, we may look for the complement of rhyme either behind or beyond us.

> When in the chronicles of wasted time
> I see descriptions of the fairest wights,
> And beauty making beautiful old rhyme,
> In praise of ladies dead and lovely knights . .

'Time—rhyme': there is no literal affinity between the two words, and yet as we hear or read them here they are united in our minds by something more than similarity of sound. Used thus in conjunction each acquires from the other an associative meaning which is drawn from the unsearchable mines of our linguistic knowledge. Of our personal share in this knowledge we are more or less consciously in control, but there is also part of it, inseparable from the rest, which derives from a racial experience which goes back to unknown beginnings. This part of our linguistic knowledge is not within our conscious control. We cannot track it to its source, nor can we explain it. But we are none the less aware of its profound significance. We cannot say why, beyond the similarity of sound, 'rhyme' is associated with 'time' by some remote yet intense activity of our minds : we only know that it is so. And it is in this associative quality in words—not, I need hardly say, in words only of a rhyme sequence— that half the secret of poetry is to be found if we could find it. That is why, with no exceptions that are not negligible, authentic poetry has never been written in any language but that to which the poet was born. A man's acquired mastery of a language that is not his mother tongue may be complete in everything but this, but of this he must fall short.

To return, then, to the sonnet. Its rhyme is more than ornamental, it is organic, for reasons which I have attempted to explain. Next, to consider the arrangement of the rhymes. Two main alternative schemes, and two alone, have been recognized and established in the practice of English poetry. One is the Italian, *a.b.b.a.a.b.b.a.* for the octave, with three rhymes for the sextet, which may be disposed variously *c.d.e.c.d.e.* or *c.d.c.e.d.e.* or *c.d.e.d.e.c.*, or, in fact, as you will, always with the strict condition that the last two lines may not rhyme. The other is English or Shakespearean, and has one invariable pattern, *a.b.a.b.c.d.c.d.e.f.e.f.g.g.* The choice between the two must always remain a matter of taste. Excellent poets have maintained, and have sought to show by example, that the austerer Italian form has a refinement of which the English is incapable. Be that as it may, the fact remains that most English poets, including those of the Shakespearean age, who were the first and are still the unsurpassed masters of the sonnet in our language, have found the greater flexibility and warmth of the native form a wider scope for the native genius, both in mood and music.

This analysis of the sonnet-form is the only discussion of the kind that I propose to make. It may help to discover principles that are generally applicable. Why, we may now ask, is the rhyme scheme of the English sonnet so satisfactory ? But first, it should be said that its flexibility or freedom does not mean that it is easy to master. On the contrary, it is a form of great difficulty, and for one particular reason. The crowning beauty of the scheme is its final couplet, and it is in the couplet that many otherwise admirable sonnets have come to grief. Successfully managed, the couplet acts as a clamp firmly tying up the whole structure. It brings melody to its perfect close, and it clinches the argument. But about this success there must be no half-measures. The couplet of an English sonnet is inevitably one of only two things : either it is splendid, or it is trivial. The smallest note of failure here, and the whole poem tumbles to ruin. How ruthlessly that note hunts the poet, those who have attempted the form know.

Why the three quatrains of alternating rhymes in six

pairs, and the closing couplet ? Why not, for example, seven couplets ? Again we approach the reason's no-man's-land, but again, perhaps, we can get a little beyond the statement that the arrangement is agreeable because it is. The rhymed couplet has been one of the mainstays of English verse since Chaucer, and it can be as fresh and new to-day as ever it was. In it the effect of rhyme is reduced to its final simplicity ; the expectancy of one line is fulfilled in the next, and no later than that. In the quatrain of alternating rhymes, on the other hand, the fulfilment is in longer suspense, and the demand made on the ear and mind is in consequence more complicated. This complication gives an added delight, but also it involves a greater strain on the perception. For a time the strain is bracing and exhilarating, but, like all other strenuous exercise, for a time only. The quatrain of alternating rhymes is a lovely thing in itself, but when used for a poem of any considerable length the effort exacted from the reader in waiting for the suspended fulfilment of his expectancy begins after a time to become exhausting, and it is a significant fact that hardly any of the major long English poems have been written in the form. The most famous, as it is also, perhaps, the most success-ful, is Gray's *Elegy*, but I sometimes wonder whether even that great work does not sometimes falter in effect for this very reason. Moreover, it must be added that the *Elegy* cannot really be called a long poem at all. Tennyson's *In Memoriam* comes nearer to our case, the four-foot as against the five-foot line making no matter. But Tennyson himself seems to have recognized the danger of which we speak, and sought to avoid it by substituting *a.b.b.a.* for *a.b.a.b.* in his rhymes. It was a cunning device. His instinct told him that the additionally prolonged delay in fulfilment from the first and fourth lines would find more than compensation in the immediate fulfilment in the third from the second, and that this compensation would indeed bring the whole nearer than alternating rhymes to the continuous ease of successive couplets. On the whole it must be allowed that his instinct was right. But he would be a very rash poet who should attempt another poem of any length in the *In Memoriam* stanza.

In a very short poem, however, the quatrain of alternating rhymes has no time to burden or weary our delight in its delicate texture. The suspended fulfilment loses none of its fresh charm, does not grow irksome. How short the poem should be is a question to which the answer must seem to be arbitrary. But the great sonneteers have shown that three quatrains is a perfect if not an incomparable choice. Less than this, it might be claimed, and we have not enough to give our pleasure its full relish ; more, and the first faint suspicion of surfeit may begin to appear. It is assessment by trial and error, but even so the proof of the notion is in the sonnet.

The effect of the concluding couplet is precisely of a piece with our theory of the general rhyme-scheme. At the end of three quatrains, on six pairs of alternating rhyme, the full effect of the arrangement has been made, neither more nor less. The poet, that is to say poetry, the whole commonwealth of poets, know that the exact moment has been reached when satisfaction may be on the point of becoming restive, and in the couplet with its immediate fulfilment standing in contrast to the preceding suspense, gives final and complete relief to all such apprehension. The art of verse has achieved no subtler convention.

Then, why the five-foot line in preference to the four, which is the other great base of English rhymed verse ? Again we can find part of our way to an answer, and part only. The cumulative poetic mind of the race has decided that in any passionate or weighty matter our language best expresses itself in a line of five iambic feet. The four-foot line has graces and melodies of its own, but it lacks something of the power and gravity that the additional foot supplies. Similarly, if we extend the five feet to six, there is an inevitable loss of compactness and precision, and the beautifully firm yet supple structure of the line is impaired. In practice the six-foot line has never been of any consequence in English verse. But the four-foot line is second only to the five in the record of things done. It is the five-foot line, however, that has appropriately been named ' heroic ', and upon it nearly all of the more spacious expression in our poetry has been framed. We may ask, beyond that, why in the shaping consciousness of our race this disposition of syllables asserted itself above all others as the fittest for the purpose, and we shall find no answer.

The five-foot line, in three quatrains of alternating lines with a closing couplet, and seven rhymes in all— we have sought, not altogether vainly I think, for reasons why the English or Shakespearean sonnet builds itself to that pattern and no other. There remains the invariable division of the fourteen lines into two sections, of eight and six lines respectively. Each of these has its own separate function to perform, and in this, as in the regulated number of lines, there is no departure from the Italian models upon which the first English sonneteers in part founded their practice. Briefly, the octave states the circumstance or argument that is to be applied with a new note of emphasis to a given occasion

in the sextet. If such distinctions are tenable at all
in poetry, we may say that it is from this process that
we derive our intellectual satisfaction in the sonnet. It
is in its nature a process of logic, and in this feature of
the sonnet we do indeed find, in the smallest compass,
as much of the delight of pure reason as in any of the
figures of poetry. When we consider all these its
elements, we see in the sonnet the grandest effects of
poetic architecture perfectly realized on a small scale.
There is nothing of majesty or of lyric tenderness or
of passion of which it is incapable.

Small wonder then that the Shakespeareans made it
their first choice when the deeper movement of love
was their theme. Examples of their success in the
earlier years of the age have been given ; others, though
few, may be set beside them from the turn of the six-
teenth century to the seventeenth. William Drum-
mond of Hawthornden, born in 1585, learned alike in
the arts and sciences, and dying, it is said, of a broken
heart when Charles the First was executed, could write :

> Sound hoarse, sad lute, true witness of my woe,
> And strive no more to ease self-chosen pain
> With soul-enchanting sounds, your accents strain
> Unto those tears incessantly which flow.
> Sad treble, weep, and you, dull basses, show
> Your master's sorrow in a doleful strain ;
> Let never joyful hand upon you go,
> Nor concert keep but when you do complain.
> Fly Phoebus' rays, abhor the irksome light ;
> Woods' solitary shades for thee are best,
> Or the black horrours of the blackest night,
> When all the world save thou and I do rest :
> Then sound, sad lute, and bear a mourning part,
> Thou Hell canst move, though not a woman's heart.

William Browne of Tavistock, born six years later
than Drummond, wrote in *Britannia's Pastorals* a
poem fragrant to the memory though rather long
to read. But some of his sonnets are not unworthy
of a poet who learnt from Spenser and influenced
Keats.

> Were't not for you, here should my pen have rest
> And take a long leave of sweet poesy ;
> Britannia's swains, and rivers far by west,
> Should hear no more mine oaten melody ;
> Yet shall the song I sung of them awhile
> Unperfect lie, and make no further known
> The happy loves of this our pleasant Isle ;
> Till I have left some record of mine own.
> You are the subject now, and, writing you,
> I well may versify, not poetize :
> Here needs no fiction : for the graces true
> And virtues clip not with base flatteries.
> > Here could I write what you deserve of praise,
> > Others might wear, but I should win the bays.

It would, however, be wanton to take leave of the love
sonnet of the age with any but its supreme master in
mind, and so we must for a moment turn back to
Shakespeare :

> Since brass, nor stone, nor earth, nor boundless sea,
> But sad mortality o'ersways their power,
> How with this rage shall beauty hold a plea,
> Whose action is no stronger than a flower ?
> O, how shall summer's honey breath hold out
> Against the wreckful siege of battering days,
> When rocks impregnable are not so stout,
> Nor gates of steel so strong, but Time decays ?

11

O fearful meditation ! where, alack,
Shall Time's best jewel from Time's chest lie hid ?
Or what strong hand can hold his swift foot back,
Or who his spoil of beauty can forbid ?
   O, none, unless this miracle have might,
   That in black ink my love may still shine bright.

And of the Elizabethan—the term will not be denied—
love lyric in general we will take leave with three
examples of the highest excellence. Their poets were
born respectively in 1568, 1573, and 1595, and so repre-
sent the full range of Shakespeare's immediate succession.
The first, Sir Henry Wotton, was, it is said, a shrewd
Ambassador ; he was also Provost of Eton ; but he
might have drifted with these titles into oblivion if he
had not written—

> You meaner beauties of the night,
>   That poorly satisfy our eyes
> More by your number than your light,
>   You common people of the skies ;
>   What are you when the moon shall rise ?

> You curious chanters of the wood,
>   That warble forth Dame Nature's lays,
> Thinking your passions understood
>   By your weak accents ; what's your praise
>   When Philomel her voice shall raise ?

> You violets that first appear,
>   By your pure purple mantles known
> Like the proud virgins of the year,
>   As if the spring were all your own ;
>   What are you when the rose is blown ?

So, when my mistress shall be seen
  In form and beauty of her mind,
By virtue first, then choice, a Queen,
  Tell me, if she were not design'd
  Th' eclipse and glory of her kind.

The second, Ben Jonson, was, if we except the promise
of Marlowe's ill-starred genius, the only dramatic poet
of an age so fabulously rich—for it has become fabled—
in dramatic poetry who really approached Shakespeare
in stature. It is hardly too much to say that as Shake-
speare was above Jonson in range of dramatic invention
and command of his instrument, so was Jonson above
all other rivals. Englishmen will never realize this until
and unless Mr. Percy Simpson and his like are heard at
the day of judgment. They do not, however, need to
be persuaded that this is a lyric masterpiece :

Drink to me only with thine eyes,
  And I will pledge with mine ;
Or leave a kiss but in the cup
  And I'll not look for wine.
The thirst that from the soul doth rise
  Doth ask a drink divine ;
But might I of Jove's nectar sup,
  I would not change for thine.

I sent thee late a rosy wreath,
  Not so much honouring thee
As giving it a hope that there
  It could not wither'd be ;
But thou thereon didst only breathe,
  And sent'st it back to me ;
Since when it grows, and smells, I swear,
  Not of itself but thee !

Thomas Carew, our third poet, was, says the *Dictionary of National Biography*, ' a man of dissipated habits '. It seems likely that he was, and in any case he died young after a questionable career in court circles. But he wrote—

> Ask me no more where Jove bestows,
> When June is past, the fading rose ;
> For in your beauty's orient deep
> These flowers, as in their causes, sleep.
>
> Ask me no more whither do stray
> The golden atoms of the day ;
> For in pure love heaven did prepare
> Those powders to enrich your hair.
>
> Ask me no more whither doth haste
> The nightingale when May is past ;
> For in your sweet dividing throat
> She winters and keeps warm her note.
>
> Ask me no more where those stars 'light
> That downwards fall in dead of night ;
> For in your eyes they sit, and there
> Fixèd become as in their sphere.
>
> Ask me no more if east or west
> The Phoenix builds her spicy nest ;
> For unto you at last she flies,
> And in your fragrant bosom dies.

It may be that Carew was not a conspicuously good man, but it is unfortunately certain that the best of men have seldom written a poem as good as that. Perhaps it is that the moralists are not always quite moral in their inferences.

Alongside Carew may be set an anonymous trifle from a miscellany published in 1602. Any of the best lyrists might have written it :

> My Love in her attire doth show her wit,
> It doth so well become her ;
> For every season she hath dressings fit,
> For Winter, Spring, and Summer.
> No beauty she doth miss
> When all her robes are on :
> But Beauty's self she is
> When all her robes are gone.

And with that again, from a similar source, another of even rarer quality :

> There is a Lady sweet and kind,
> Was never face so pleased my mind ;
> I did but see her passing by,
> And yet I love her till I die.
>
> Her gesture, motion, and her smiles,
> Her wit, her voice my heart beguiles,
> Beguiles my heart, I know not why,
> And yet I love her till I die.
>
> Cupid is wingèd and doth range,
> Her country so my love doth change :
> But change she earth, or change she sky,
> Yet will I love her till I die.

One other poet of the age, John Donne, made love a great lyric theme. But he is for our later thought.

X

ELIZABETHAN LYRIC

OTHER THEMES

LOVE as a lyric theme of the time outdid all comparison. Even age and mortality, nearest in approach, inspired few though fine songs. Walter Raleigh, twelve years older than Shakespeare, and the sorriest victim of faction in a factious age, left a few lines that caught—or set—the characteristic note perfectly :

> Even such is Time, that takes in trust
>   Our youth, our joys, our all we have,
> And pays us but with earth and dust ;
>   Who in the dark and silent grave,
> When we have wander'd all our ways,
> Shuts up the story of our days ;
> But from this earth, this grave, this dust,
> My God shall raise me up, I trust.

Coleridge, I think, must have remembered that when he wrote of Sir Arthur O'Kellyn—

> The Knight's bones are dust,
> And his good sword rust ;
> His soul is with the saints, I trust.

George Peele, also older than Shakespeare, and also, it is said, like Carew, of dissipated habits, celebrated the

retirement of one of Elizabeth's pensioners, who prob-
ably did not get a pension, in verses that ' make beautiful
old age ' :

His golden locks Time hath to silver turn'd ;
  O Time too swift, O swiftness never ceasing !
His youth 'gainst time and age hath ever spurn'd,
  But spurn'd in vain ; youth waneth by increasing :
Beauty, strength, youth, are flowers but fading seen ;
Duty, faith, love, are roots, and ever green.

His helmet now shall make a hive for bees ;
  And, lovers' sonnets turn'd to holy psalms,
A man-at-arms must now serve on his knees,
  And feed on prayers, which are Age his alms :
But though from court to cottage he depart,
His Saint is sure of his unspotted heart.

And when he saddest sits in homely cell,
  He'll teach his swains this carol for a song,—
' Blest be the hearts that wish my sovereign well,
  Curst be the souls that think her any wrong.'
Goddess, allow this agèd man his right
To be your beadsman now that was your knight.

Shakespeare himself was never more deeply moved in
lyric than when he wrote :

Fear no more the heat o' the sun,
  Nor the furious winter's rages ;
Thou thy worldly task hast done,
  Home art gone, and ta'en thy wages :
Golden lads and girls all must,
As chimney-sweepers, come to dust.

Fear no more the frown o' the great,
　　Thou art past the tyrant's stroke ;
Care no more to clothe and eat ;
　　To thee the reed is as the oak :
The sceptre, learning, physic, must
All follow this, and come to dust.

Fear no more the lightning-flash,
　　Nor the all-dreaded thunder-stone ;
Fear not slander, censure rash ;
　　Thou hast finish'd joy and moan :
All lovers young, all lovers must
Consign to thee, and come to dust.

Sir John Beaumont, who had the good fortune in 1592
to be born at Grace-Dieu in Leicestershire, but died at
the age of forty-six on account of something his care
for which, according to Michael Drayton, was, obscurely,
not worth his breath, and so ' brought on too soon his
much lamented death ', himself lamented the death of
a little son, Gervase, in an epitaph of very moving
poignancy :

Can I, who have for others oft compil'd
The songs of death, forget my sweetest child,
Which, like a flow'r crusht, with a blast is dead,
And ere full time hangs downe his smiling head,
Expecting with cleare hope to live anew,
Among the angels fed with heav'ny dew ?
We have this signe of joy, that many dayes,
While on the Earth his struggling spirit stayes,
The name of Jesus in his mouth containes,
His onely food, his sleepe, his ease from paines,
O may that sound be rooted in my mind,
Of which in him such strong effect I find.
Dear Lord, receive my sonne, whose winning love
To me was like a friendship, farre above

The course of nature, or his tender age,
Whose lookes could all my bitter griefes assuage ;
Let his pure soule, ordain'd sev'n yeeres to be
In that fraile body, which was part of me,
Remaine my pledge in Heav'n, as sent to shew,
How to his port at ev'ry step I goe.

John Beaumont, who wrote a spirited short-long poem
about Bosworth Field, although he died early, outlived
his younger and more famous brother Francis, for whom
also he wrote memorial lines, less tender, but still
enriched a good deal above formal compliment :

On Death, thy murd'rer, this revenge I take ;
I slight his terrour, and just question make,
Which of us two the best precedence have,
Mine to this wretched world, thine to the grave :
Thou shouldst have followed me, but Death too blame,
Miscounted yeeres, and measur'd age by fame,
So dearely hast thou bought thy precious lines,
Their praise grew swiftly ; so thy life declines :
Thy Muse, the hearer's queene, thy reader's love,
All eares, all hearts, (but Death's) could please and move.

It was Francis Beaumont himself who, with the excep-
tion of Shakespeare and one other, in his time best
epitomized mortality in a verse.

ON THE TOMBES IN WESTMINSTER

Mortality, behold, and feare
What a change of flech is here !
Thinke how many royall bones
Sleep within these heap of stones ;
Here they lye, had realmes, and lands
Who now want strength to stir their hands ;
Where from their pulpits seal'd with dust,
They preach, ' In greatnesse is no trust.'

Here's an acre sown indeed,
With the richest, royall'st seed,
That the earth did e're suck in,
Since the first man dy'd for sin :
Here the bones of birth have cry'd,
' Though Gods they were, as men they dy'd : '
Here are sands, ignoble things,
Dropt from the ruin'd sides of kings,
  Here's a world of pomp and state
  Buried in dust, once dead by fate.

The exception above noted with Shakespeare is James Shirley, who, strictly speaking, takes us out of the Elizabethan era altogether. Born in 1596, he lived through the civil wars and the Commonwealth, saw the Restoration, and died at the age of seventy. Nevertheless he was a leading figure among the dramatic poets who carried the tradition of the Elizabethan theatre on into its twilight and eclipse. He only just managed to be Elizabethan by birth, but he stood with some authority for the Shakespearean tradition in Milton's age. His lyric masterpiece, by which Cromwell is said to have been deeply affected, was probably written in the later part of his life. It was not published until 1659, but its mood is of an earlier date. Shakespeare might have written it, but not Milton :

  The glories of our blood and state
    Are shadows, not substantial things ;
  There is no armour against Fate ;
    Death lays his icy hand on kings :
      Sceptre and Crown
      Must tumble down,
  And in the dust be equal made
  With the poor crookèd scythe and spade.

Some men with swords may reap the field,
  And plant fresh laurels where they kill :
But their strong nerves at last must yield ;
  They tame but one another still :
      Early or late
      They stoop to fate,
And must give up their murmuring breath
When they, pale captives, creep to death.

The garlands wither on your brow ;
  Then boast no more your mighty deeds !
Upon Death's purple altar now
  See where the victor-victim bleeds.
      Your heads must come
      To the cold tomb :
Only the actions of the just
Smell sweet and blossom in their dust.

Another theme of some favour among the Elizabethan
lyrists was that of courtly compliment. The theme
of such a poem as Henry Wotton's to His Mistress
the Queen of Bohemia, which has been quoted, was
something deeper than that, and places it legitimately
among the love lyrics of the age. A good example
of the specifically Court lyric is this, by Sir John
Davies :

TO THE NIGHTINGALE

Ev'ry night from ev'n to morn,
Love's chorister amid the thorn
Is now so sweet a singer,
So sweet, as for her song I scorn
Apollo's voice and finger.

But Nightingale, sith you delight
Ever to watch the starry night,
Tell all the stars of Heaven,
Heaven never had a star so bright,
As now to Earth is given.

Royal Astrea makes our day
Eternal with her beams, nor may
Gross darkness overcome her ;
I now perceive why some do write,
No country hath so short a night,
As England hath in summer.

Davies, born of a good Wiltshire family in 1570, was expelled from the Middle Temple for beating a fellow member in Hall, survived the disgrace, and became Attorney-General in Ireland with subsequent advancement to the bench. He wrote a long poem on dancing, called *Orchestra*, which unexpectedly is a really splendid exercise in rhyme royal, and another, in quatrains, on The Immortality of the Soul, which is less inviting. He also wrote *Hymns of Astrea*, twenty-six in number, of which the above is one. Astrea was Elizabeth, and it will be seen that the verses form an acrostic of the words Elisabetha Regina. He repeats this feat in every poem of the series. It is astonishing that a poet could have thought it worth while to do this, but even more astonishing that he should have done it with so little appearance of constraint. Hardly ever do his self-imposed and rather ridiculous fetters hamper his movement or in any way embarrass a very charming natural grace. The little work as a whole is no better for being a *tour de force*, but against all the odds it is certainly no worse.

One other poet calls for mention before we pass from one age to another by means of John Donne, who belonged to both and yet was very much his own man. This is Richard Corbet, who was born in 1582, became Bishop of Oxford at the age of thirty-seven and of Norwich at forty, in spite of some reputation for levity thought to be unbecoming his cloth. He entertained Ben Jonson at Oxford when the great dramatist was given a degree, which was a distinguished thing to do, and when he died at the age of forty-three, it was written of him ' he loved to the last boy's play very well ', which was a distinguished epitaph to earn. He must have been an attractive if disconcerting bishop. Being thrown out of a coach with a fat friend, Dr. Stubbins, in a very dirty lane, he said that Dr. Stubbins was up to the elbows in mud, and he was up to the elbows in Stubbins. His reputation as a poet has been curious. He was a satirist—anti-Puritan—of some power, and he could write a lyric as charming as this one to his son Vincent on his third birthday :

> What I shall leave thee none can tell,
> But all shall say I wish thee well ;
> I wish thee, Vin, before all wealth,
> Both bodily and ghostly health :
> Nor too much wealth, nor wit, come to thee,
> So much of either may undo thee.
> I wish thee learning, not for show,
> Enough for to instruct, and know ;
> Not such as gentlemen require,
> To prate at table, or at fire.
> I wish thee all thy mother's graces,
> Thy father's fortunes, and his places.
> I wish thee friends, and one at court,
> Not to build on, but support ;

To keep thee, not in doing many
Oppressions, but from suffering any.
I wish thee peace in all thy wayes,
Nor lazy nor contentious days ;
And when thy soul and body part,
As innocent as now thou art.

His poems were not printed until twelve years after his death, and then, enjoying some popularity for a time, they fell out of notice until Chalmers included them in his great collection in 1810. I know of no later edition. They find no place in *The Golden Treasury* nor in the *Oxford Book of English Verse*, and they are not mentioned by Courthope. And yet Corbet wrote one of the best-known lines in the language, ' Farewell rewards and Faeries ', which was familiar long before Mr. Kipling borrowed from it. But for a hundred people who know it I don't suppose there are three who could give the next or any other line of the poem. And it is a poem of quite remarkable quality, unlike anything else of its own age, and difficult to match with a true fellow from any.

A PROPER NEW BALLAD,

INTITULED

THE FAERYE'S FAREWELL ;

OR

GOD-A-MERCY WILL

(To be sung or whistled to the tune of ' The Meddow Brow ', by the learned ; by the unlearned, to the tune of ' Fortune ')

Farewell rewards and Faeries,
Good houswives now may say,
For now foule slutts in daries
Doe fare as well as they.

And though they sweepe theyr hearths no less
  Then maydes were wont to doe,
Yet who of late for cleaneliness,
  Finds sixe-pence in her shoe?

Lament, lament, old abbies,
  The Faries lost command;
They did but change priests' babies,
  But some have chang'd your land;
And all your children sprung from thence
  Are now growne Puritanes;
Who live as changelings ever since
  For love of your demaines.

At morning and at evening both
  You merry were and glad,
So little care of sleepe or sloth
  These prettie ladies had;
When Tom came home from labour,
  Or Ciss to milking rose,
Then merrily merrily went theyre tabor,
  And nimbly went theyre toes.

Wittness those rings and roundelayes
  Of theirs, which yet remaine,
Were footed in queene Marie's dayes
  On many a grassy playne;
But since of late, Elizabeth,
  And later, James came in,
They never daunc'd on any heath
  As when the time hath bin.

By which we note the Faries
  Were of the old profession;
Theyre songs were Ave Maryes;
  Theyre daunces were procession:

But now, alas ! they all are dead,
  Or gone beyond the seas ;
Or farther for religion fled,
  Or elce they take theyre ease.

A tell-tale in theyre company
  They never could endure,
And whoe so kept not secretly
  Theyre mirth was punisht sure ;
It was a just and christian deed
  To pinch such blacke and blew :
O how the common welth doth need
  Such justices as you !

There are three more stanzas, but the poem really ends
there. It is as pretty a piece of lyric scolding as is to
be found in English poetry.

John Donne was born in 1573, nine years after Shake-
speare. After a romantic youth, complicated by an
adoring marriage and a father-in-law framed in the
best transpontine manner, he took holy orders when
he was forty, became Dean of St. Paul's, and died ten
years later, in 1631. It is probable that most if not all
of his poems were written in the early part of his life ;
all the best of them, according to Ben Jonson, before
he was twenty-five. They were not published until
1633, two years after his death, but for some time before
that they had established his reputation in manuscript as
one of the most considerable poets of his age.

In date, then, Donne was an Elizabethan poet entirely.
In poetic character, however, he had small affinity with
any of his great contemporaries. His passion was steeped
in an intellectual quality that was wholly foreign to
their nature. Thought is not the governing element
in poetry, but it may be an extremely powerful one.

It may seem the merest absurdity to say that the poets of whom Shakespeare was the master did not think, but if we regard them in Donne's company it has some semblance of plausibility. The fundamental brain-work of which Rossetti was to speak three hundred years later as being essential to poetry was fused by Shakespeare and his fellows in an overwhelming faculty for perception, a creative impetus that achieved intellectual truth, as Keats divined, in an unreasoning acceptance of beauty. The intellectual power of Shakespeare's sonnets, for example, is an abiding wonder of the human mind, but it is instinctive rather than deliberate. Even Ben Jonson, the most intellectual poet of them all, swept his thought along on a torrent of verse where it thundered or sang itself into submission. Donne's thought, unlike that of all the others, was never submissive to his poetry.

In this lie at once his distinction and his difficulty. His distinction is above opinion. No one could reasonably place him with the very greatest poets in the language, but he has strong claims to be reckoned among the most original. There is hardly another English poet whose work is so unmistakably recognizable at sight. He wrote like nobody else in his time, and nobody has written like him since, or ever will. And the secret, so far as I can discover it, is that his thought . . .

XI

POETRY AND DOGMA

ARTHUR SKEMP MEMORIAL LECTURE

Delivered in the University of Bristol, January 29, 1931

LET me first try to give some indication of the sense in which the word Dogma is used in the title of this paper. It is a word defined variously in the dictionaries as 'a settled opinion', 'a principle or tenet', 'a doctrine laid down with authority, as by a church, school of philosophy, or the like', and 'a definitive, established, and authoritative tenet'. Mr. Chesterton once in controversy, I think it was with Mr. Shaw, asserted that his disputant and he, both having minds of their own, were both inevitably and properly dogmatic, the difference being that while he was dogmatic and right, Mr. Shaw was dogmatic and wrong. Which directs us to yet another dictionary definition which alleges dogma to be 'a doctrinal notion asserted without regard to evidence or truth; an arbitrary dictum'. Dogma may mean that if you like to take it so, but the significance here has been degraded. True, even the dogma to which respectable authority is attributed may be mistaken, but the mistake is of a nature other than that implied by the substitution of arbitrary for authoritative. If I assert roundly that free trade is a better policy for this country than protection, I am being dogmatic and I may be mistaken, but I can at least advance a good deal of difficult evidence in support of my view. On the other hand, when Mr. T. S. Eliot says of *Hamlet* : ' So far from being Shakespeare's masterpiece, the play is most certainly an artistic failure ', he is being dogmatic, he is mistaken, and he has no evidence whatever of the smallest consequence to advance in defence of his error. The dogmatism here is merely arbitrary. It may be true that the critic has evolved an aesthetic theory that leads him to the conclusion that *Hamlet* is most certainly an artistic failure, but there was once a community which held enthusiastically to a theory which proved the moon to be a cheese.

For present purposes, let me define dogma as a passionate belief that is neither founded on manifest error, nor wholly indisputable in its terms. It is neither blind self-deception, such as the ' I am bound to win ' of the pugilist, nor is it an announcement of plain fact, such as ' Two and two make four '. To elevate the examples, we might instance the doctrine that by one church only may a man's soul be saved, and the affirmation that fire burns. The doctrine which, in spite of all priestly persuasion, relates to something that is definitely beyond human experience, to what is doubtless a reality, but a reality which no human faculty can perceive, and the affirmation which relates to a physical fact that unphilosophically may be called self-evident, may both come within the scope of poetry, but neither is dogmatic within our present meaning.

We may as well clear the issue still further by admitting at once that our dogma is far less associated with religious speculation or physical science than with morals. The passionate faith of which I have spoken

is commonly a faith in the virtue of some moral code
as applied to the conduct of life. To start off with a
quite simple example, there are certain people who do
genuinely believe in the wisdom of the precept : 'Judge
not, that ye be not judged'. They do not take this
as ordaining that they should not form opinions about
other people's conduct, but rather that it is a sounder
social and spiritual economy to look for good motives
than for bad as the springs of any human action. The
quest may sometimes be unrewarded, but with such
people it will always in the first place at least be under-
taken. This disposition is figuratively a clause in a moral
code. And it is one that is observed by certain people
with great determination. Their belief in its virtue
amounts, in fact, to dogmatism. And it is dogmatism
of this nature of which I speak. The inquiry which I
wish to make in this paper is whether such dogmatism
should be utilized by or excluded from the poet's activity.

At first sight it would seem that the best witnesses
are for exclusion. In modern criticism, especially, there
has been a frequent insistence on the integrity of poetry
in itself, of what is sometimes called pure poetry. I
ask your indulgence while I quote at some length words
that I myself published a good many years ago.[1]

The question that naturally follows these reflections is—
Are there degrees in poetry ? Since a short lyric may
completely satisfy the requirements of poetry as here set
down, announcing itself to have been created in a poetic or
supremely intensified mood, can poetry be said at any time
to go beyond this ? If we accept these conclusions, can a
thing so slight, yet so exquisite, so obviously authentic in
source as :

---

[1] *The Lyric*, Martin Secker, 1915.

When I a verse shall make,
  Know I have pray'd thee,
For old religion's sake,
  Saint Ben, to aid me.

Make the way smooth for me,
  When I, thy Herrick,
Honouring thee, on my knee
  Offer my lyric.

Candles I'll give to thee,
  And a new altar,
And thou, Saint Ben, shall be
  Writ in my Psalter,

be said to be less definitely poetry than *Paradise Lost* or in any
essentially poetic way below it ? The logical answer is No ;
and I think it is the right one. In considering it we should
come to an understanding of the nature of lyric, the purpose
of this essay. But first let us see how far it may be justifiable.

It is commonly asserted and accepted that *Paradise Lost* is
among the two or three greatest English poems ; it may
justly be taken as the type of supreme poetic achievement
in our literature. What are the qualities by virtue of which
this claim is made, and allowed by every competent judge ?
Firstly, there is the witness of that ecstasy of mood of which
we have spoken :

His praise, ye Winds, that from four quarters blow,
Breathe soft or loud : and wave your tops, ye Pines,
With every plant, in sign of worship wave.
Fountains, and ye that warble, as ye flow,
Melodious murmurs, warbling tune his praise.
Join voices, all ye living souls. Ye Birds,
That, singing, up to Heaven-gate ascend,
Bear on your wings and in your notes his praise.
Ye that in waters glide, and ye that walk
The earth, and stately tread, or lowly creep,
Witness if I be silent, morn or even,
To hill or valley, fountain, or fresh shade,
Made vocal by my song, and taught his praise.

This note of high imaginative tension is persistent throughout the poem, and that it should be so masterfully sustained is in itself cause for delighted admiration. But to be constant in a virtue is not to enhance its quality. Superbly furnished as *Paradise Lost* is with this imaginative beauty, the beauty is as rich and unquestionable in the few pages of *Lycidas*; there is less of it, that is all. And who shall say that it is less ecstatic or less perfect in the little orison to Saint Ben? You may prefer Milton's manner, but then you may, with equal reason, prefer Herrick's, being grateful for what Keats announced to be truth, in whatever shape you may find it. In any case we cannot, on this ground, assign a lower place to the poet who could order those words ' religion's ', ' Saint Ben ', ' Psalter ', and the rest of them, with such inspired good fortune. And yet we know that *Paradise Lost* is a greater work than this little flight of certain song, greater, too, than the poet's own elegy. There is an explanation.

Of all the energies of man, that which I will anticipate my argument by calling the poetic energy, the energy that created Herrick's song and the distinguishing qualities of that passage from Milton, is the rarest and the most highly, if not the most generally, honoured; we have only to think of the handful of men who at any time out of all the millions can bring this perfect expression to a mood of the highest imaginative intensity, to know that the honour is justly bestowed. So splendid a thing is success in this matter that failure, if it is matched with a will for sincerity and intelligence of purpose, will often bring a man some durable fame. But the energies of man are manifold, and while we rightly set the poetic energy above the rest, there are others which are only less rare, and in their most notable manifestations yielding to it alone in worthiness of homage which will, indeed, often be more generally paid. Such an energy is the profound intellectual control of material, as distinct from profound emotional sensitiveness to material; the capacity for ordering great masses of detail into a whole of finely-balanced and duly-related proportions. Caesar and Napoleon had it, marshalling great armies to perfectly conceived designs ; Fielding had it, using it to draw a multitude of character and event into the superbly shaped lines of his story ; the greatest political leaders have had it ; Cromwell had it, organizing an enthusiasm ; Elizabeth, organizing a national adventure. Again, there is the energy of morality, ardently desiring justice and right fellowship, sublimely lived by men who have made goodness great, like Lincoln, sublimely spoken by men who made sermons passionate, like Ruskin and Carlyle. To take one other instance, there is the highly-specialized energy that delights in the objective perception of differentiations of character, the chief energy of the deftest wits, such as Samuel Johnson and the best comic dramatists.

Any one of these energies, greatly manifested, will compel a just admiration ; not so great an admiration as the poetic energy, which is witness of the highest urgency of individual life, of all things the most admirable, but still great. If, further, we consider any one of these energies by itself, we shall see that if it were co-existent with the poetic energy, the result would be likely to be that, in contact with so masterful a force, it would become yet more emphatic, and so a thing arresting in itself would become yet more notable under its new dominion. And so it is. Fielding's architectural power is a yet more wonderful thing in Sophocles, where it is allied to poetic energy ; Ruskin's moral fervour is, for all its nobility, less memorable than Wordsworth's, and Ben Jonson defines character more pungently than Sheridan. These energies remain, nevertheless, distinct from the poetic energy. When, however, a poet is endowed not alone with his own particular gift of poetry, but also with some of these other energies—of which there are many—his work very rightly is allowed an added greatness. It is so with *Paradise Lost*. Of the three energies other than the poetic that I have mentioned, Milton had rich measure of two and something of the third. No man has ever excelled him either in power of intellectual control or in moral passion, and he was not without some sense of character. Consequently we get

in his great poem, not only the dominating poetic quality
which is the chief thing, enabling the poet to realize his vision
(or mood) perfectly, but also the spectacle of a great number
of perfectly realized visions being related to each other with
excellent harmony ; we get, further, a great moral exultation
—again perfectly realized by the poetic energy, and we get,
finally, considerable subtlety—far more than is generally
allowed—of psychological detail. From all these things, the
architectonics, the zeal for justice and the revelation of
character, we get an added and wholesome delight which
give Milton's work a place of definitely greater eminence
than Herrick's song in the record of human activity. In
effect, Milton, besides being a poet, which is the greatest of
all distinctions, becomes, by possession of those other qualities,
a great man as well, and I think that this is really what we
mean when we speak of a great poet. Without his poetic
faculty, although he would fall in the scale of human distinc-
tion, which is not at all the same thing as renown, below,
say, so humble a personality yet so true a poet as John Clare,
Milton would still be a great man, while Herrick without
his poetry would be indistinguishable from the crowd. And
the great man is as clearly evident in Milton's poetry as he
is clearly not evident in Herrick's.

It is fifteen years since I wrote that, and I repeat it
now from a book no longer easily accessible, not so
much for the argument in itself, as to show that I am
fully sensible of any claims that may be put in for
pure poetry. I still find it difficult to discern the poetic
essence more readily in *Paradise Lost* than in Herrick's
little prayer. *Paradise Lost* was more difficult to write,
because to the prime difficulty there were many other
and important difficulties added ; but the prime difficulty
in each case was the same, and in each case as unlikely
of conquest. A blank sheet and a pen—with nothing
but these, the transfiguration into ' Of man's first dis-

obedience and the fruit' was no less probable than
that into 'When I a verse shall make'. The authority
of 'pure poetry', then, is not disputed.

But even so, what are the origins of this 'pure
poetry'? Let us concede so much to abstraction, that
very dangerous lure, as to allow that chief among
them is that inspiration of which the nature and secret
have escaped the most vigilant moods of definition.
Grant the inspiration, still it is faced with the necessity
of finding material upon which to work, and at this
point the critical mind can no longer take refuge in
abstraction. Inspiration, whatever it may be, must be
sterile or fulfil itself by an occasion. The occasion must
be definite and definable, and criticism not only can
but must be aware of the nature of this. In other words,
we cannot escape the responsibility of determining what
poetry does, though we may confess our inability to
explain how poetry contrives to do it.

The material upon which the inspired poetic faculty
works would appear to be secure against any malapert
classification, since it is as diffuse and universal as life
itself. Anc. yet, for our purpose, the attempt must be
made, and, in fact, a good deal more hopefully than
might be supposed. The infinite detail of life that is
absorbed and expressed by poetry can be catalogued
only by the whole body of poetry itself, but on reflection
we shall find this detail arranging itself with unexpected
ease into certain generalized groups of experience. I
will be more specific, and say these groups are three in
number.

1. The material in the first group consists of im-
pressions made directly upon the poet's mind by natural

objects, by objective action, and by personal sensation, all
recorded without philosophic argument.   Examples are :

a

Therefore all seasons shall be sweet to thee,
Whether the summer clothe the general earth
With greenness, or the redbreast sit and sing
Betwixt the tufts of snow on the bare branch
Of mossy apple-tree, while the nigh thatch
Smokes in the sun-thaw ; whether the evedrops fall,
Heard only in the trances of the blast,
Or if the secret ministry of frost
Shall hang them up in silent icicles,
Quietly shining to the quiet moon.

b

Alone stood brave Horatius,
    But constant still in mind ;
Thrice thirty thousand foes before,
    And the broad flood behind.
' Down with him ! ' cried false Sextus,
    With a smile on his pale face.
' Now yield thee,' cried Lars Porsena,
    ' Now yield thee to our grace.'

Round turned he, as not deigning
    Those craven ranks to see ;
Nought spake he to Lars Porsena,
    To Sextus nought spake he ;
But he saw on Palatinus
    The white porch of his home ;
And spake to the noble river
    That rolls by the towers of Rome.

' Oh, Tiber ! father Tiber !
    To whom the Romans pray,
A Roman's life, a Roman's arms,
    Take thou in charge this day ! '

So he spake, and speaking sheathed
  The good sword by his side,
And with his harness on his back,
  Plunged headlong in the tide.

c

Whate'er the theme, the Maiden sang
As if her song could have no ending ;
I saw her singing at her work,
And o'er the sickle bending ;—
I listened, motionless and still ;
And, as I mounted up the hill,
The music in my heart I bore,
Long after it was heard no more.

2. The second group consists of material which shows
these various impressions not merely recorded, but re-
corded in their effect upon the poet's emotion.   He does
not here apply it to a moral code, but he appropriates
it to the activity of his own feelings.   Poetry is pro-
fuse in the employment of such material, and a large
anthology of examples could readily be compiled :

a

O, that a man might know
The end of this day's business ere it come !
But it sufficeth that the day will end,
And then the end is known.

b

But at my back I alwaies hear
Times winged Charriot hurrying near ;
And yonder all before us lye
Desarts of vast Eternity.
Thy Beauty shall no more be found ;
Nor, in thy marble Vault, shall sound

My ecchoing Song : then Worms shall try
That long preserv'd Virginity ;
And your quaint Honour turn to dust ;
And into ashes all my Lust.
The Grave's a fine and private place,
But none I think do there embrace.

c

He has outsoared the shadow of our night ;
Envy and calumny and hate and pain,
And that unrest which men miscall delight,
Can touch him not and torture not again ;
From the contagion of the world's slow stain
He is secure, and now can never mourn
A heart grown cold, a head grown gray in vain ;
Nor, when the spirit's self has ceased to burn
With sparkless ashes load an unlamented urn.

3. The third group brings us to the heart of the
present question. It consists of material in which the
poet goes beyond the record of an object or action, and
beyond the record of its effect upon his emotions, and
allows himself to embellish the occasion with dogmatic
statement or reflection of the kind that has been indicated.
The fitness of this practice seems, as I have said, to have
been repudiated by many whose testimony is entitled
to respect. It is almost a commonplace of criticism
that poetry must not preach. And yet I think that
criticism has here fallen into some confusion. Quite
recently Mr. John Livingston Lowes, the very acute
American critic who was appointed to the first tenure
of the Eastman Foundation in the University of Oxford,
wrote : ' So soon as he moralizes, the poet has abdicated
his throne.' In support of this contention he was able
to cite Keats with ' We hate poetry that has a palpable

design upon us '. When Keats says anything about poetry we have to listen, and although I am not sure that these words in their context bear quite the meaning that Mr. Lowes attributes to them in aligning them with his own about the poet's abdication, we may allow that Keats's intention was directed in general against moralizing poetry. But the unquestionable truth that may be conceded to Keats and Mr. Lowes has very commonly been used to press the argument a good deal beyond its legitimate limits. Mr. Lowes himself shows an inclination to do this. It will be noticed that the design which Keats stigmatizes as being offensive is a palpable design. Mr. Lowes would seem to accept this condition.

Poetry [he says] may teach, then, if it teaches in art's way—if, in Browning's phrase, it ' does the thing shall breed the thought '. ' To instruct delightfully,' says Dryden, following Sir Philip Sydney, ' is the general end of all poetry. Philosophy instructs, but it performs its work by precept, which is not delightful, or not so delightful as example.' Browning and Dryden are at one ; the poet's business is not with precept. The teacher's and the preacher's is—though not so much, I shrewdly suspect, as they suppose. Poetry does not teach us, but it allows us to be taught, as life and the universe permit us, if we will, to learn. The poet's sense of ethical values, if he has it, may communicate itself to us, as Shakespeare's does, implicitly, without the intrusion of a moral sentiment.

Here, indeed, is a cloud of witnesses, but the testimony remains inconclusive. To allow that the poet may have a design upon us so long as it is not palpable, to admit that he may indulge his sense of ethical values so long as he does not make a spectacle of it, to commend example as against precept—all this is all very well, but I cannot find from my knowledge of poetry that the poets of any consequence, so splendidly many of them, have ever been in serious danger of this kind of transgression. The poet is a very proud being, very sure of his mission and of the dignity of his art. But it is characteristic of him also that he is philosophically humble. Sycophant he must never be, which is quite another matter. He may denounce abuses and scold tyrants, but these occasions in no way affect his essential humility. However deadly his invective may be when provoked by particular wrong, it is a mark of his vocation that he has in the general conduct of life a settled distaste for interfering with other people's business. In his heightened sensibility he knows too well the fallibility of his own judgements, the insecurity of his own motives, and the caprices of his own behaviour, to assume magisterial manners towards the rest of the world. He has, in fact, even though no trace of it should appear in his poetry, a sense of humour which in these matters saves him from the errors of disproportion. And so, of all people he is the least likely to assume the office of pedagogue in general to the world. In fact, the offence against which the poet is warned by Mr. Lowes and, he can claim, by an imposing bench of poets in session, is one into which by the ample evidence of poetry itself the poet shows no disposition to fall.

And yet the terms of the caution are such that they have suffered a general and serious misapplication. The admonishment that he must not do something which he has no intention of doing has been commonly construed as a censure of something else that has been constantly in his practice. In general, the poet becomes tiresome, and even ridiculous, when he presumes to instruct other people in the application of moral principles. We may allow him a little latitude in satire, or in the correction of some particular or notorious abuse, but there we stop. In the wider scope of his work we will not have the poet telling us how to behave. This is a conclusion upon which Mr. Lowes and the rest must be insisting, but it is a conclusion which can never have been in any reasonable doubt. It is, indeed, difficult to understand how it ever came into dispute. If that were all, we could pass it by as being of no great matter, reflecting merely that by some caprice the poets had made a strange critical ado about the obvious. But it is not all.

For the obvious is here of so elementary a nature, that our minds have formed a nebulous impression that all this critical thunder could not have been directed, with the assistance of the poets themselves, against so easy and defenceless a mark. And a common belief has arisen that under the censure of these authorities has fallen not only any palpable design in the poet to direct other people in this application of moral principles, but any palpable display of moral principles in his own preoccupations. In forbidding him to be dogmatic to the tune of telling us how faith should be justified in our acts, the court, whether intentionally or not, has appeared to forbid him also the other dogmatism of declaring what faith he would wish to be served.

The critics, many poets among them, have in this gone far towards throwing one aspect of poetic theory into confusion. Many cultivated readers of poetry, if asked at a venture whether moral dogmatism was a fitting exercise of the poetic faculty, would reply No, in the belief that their answer was confirmed by the main body of established critical opinion. The answer would be wholly misguided. For moral dogmatism, within our intention, has been steadily within the practice of the poets themselves, and not least within the practice of those poets who are cited as testifying against it. Let us see. The names just given by Mr. Lowes are Browning, Dryden, Sydney, Keats.

> Let men
> Regard me, and the poet dead long ago
> Who loved too rashly ; and shape forth a third
> And better-tempered spirit, warned by both :
> As from the over-radiant star too mad
> To drink the life-springs, beamless thence itself—
> And the dark orb which borders the abyss,
> Ingulfed in icy night,—might have its course
> A temperate and equidistant world.
> Meanwhile, I have done well, though not all well
> As yet men cannot do without contempt ;
> 'Tis for their good, and therefore fit awhile
> That they reject the weak, and scorn the false,
> Rather than praise the strong and true, in me :
> But after, they will know me. If I stoop
> Into a dark tremendous sea of cloud,
> It is but for a time ; I press God's lamp
> Close to my breast ; its splendour, soon or late,
> Will pierce the gloom : I shall emerge one day.

> Then off made buyer with a prize,
>   Then seller to his *Times* returned
> And so did day wear, wear, till eyes
>   Brightened apace, for rest was earned :
>   He locked door long ere candle burned.

> And whither went he ? Ask himself,
>   Not me ! To change of scene, I think.
> Once sold the ware and pursed the pelf,
>   Chaffer was scarce his meat and drink,
>   Nor all his music—money-chink.

Because a man has shop to mind
   In time and place, since flesh must live,
Needs spirit lack all life behind,
   All stray thoughts, fancies fugitive,
   All loves except what trade can give ?

I want to know a butcher paints,
   A baker rhymes for his pursuit,
Candlestick-maker much acquaints
   His soul with song, or, haply mute,
   Blows out his brains upon the flute !

But—shop each day and all day long !
   Friend, your good angel slept, your star
Suffered eclipse, fate did you wrong !
   From where these sorts of treasures are,
   There should our heart be—Christ, how far !

Browning in these passages is clearly paying little heed
to his own precept quoted by Mr. Lowes from a passage
at the conclusion of *The Ring and The Book* :

Because it is the glory and good of Art,
That Art remains the one way possible
Of speaking truth, to mouths like mine at least.
How look a brother in the face and say
' Thy right is wrong, eyes hast thou yet art blind.
Thine ears are stuffed and stopped, despite their length :
And, oh, the foolishness thou countest faith ! '
      .   .   .   .   .   .
But Art,—wherein man nowise speaks to men,
Only to mankind,—Art may tell a truth
Obliquely, do the thing shall breed the thought,
Nor wrong the thought, missing the mediate word.

And although in such a poem as *Religio Laici* Dryden
may be true to his own ideal of instructing delightfully,
he can hardly claim that he is instructing by example

13

rather than precept. The argument, which passes to an
examination of deism and then of revealed religion,
opens thus :

> Dim, as the borrow'd beams of Moon and Stars
> To lonely, weary, wandring Travellers
> Is reason to the Soul : And as on high
> Those rowling Fires discover but the Sky
> Not light us here ; So Reason's glimmering Ray
> Was lent, not to assure our doubtfull way,
> But guide us upward to a better Day.
> And as those nightly Tapers disappear
> When Day's bright Lord ascends our Hemisphere ;
> So pale grows Reason at Religious sight ;
> So dyes, and so dissolves in Supernatural Light.
> Some few, whose Lamp shone brighter, have been led
> From Cause to Cause to Natures secret head ;
> And found that one first principle must be ;
> But what, or who, that Universal He ;
> Whether some Soul incompassing this Ball,
> Unmade, unmov'd ; yet making, moving All ;
> Or various Atom's, interfering Dance
> Leapt into Form (the Noble work of Chance,)
> Or this great All was from Eternity ;
> Not ev'n the Stagirite himself could see ;
> And Epicurus Guess'd as well as He.
> As blindly grop'd they for a future State,
> As rashly Judg'd of Providence and Fate :
> But least of all could their Endeavours find
> What most concern'd the good of Humane kind :
> For Happiness was never to be found :
> But vanish'd from 'em, like Enchanted ground.
> One thought Content the Good to be enjoyed :
> This, every little Accident destroyed :
> The wiser Madmen did for Vertue toyl,
> A Thorny, or at best a barren Soil :
> In Pleasure some their glutton Souls would steep,

But found their Line too short, the Well too deep,
And leaky Vessels which no Bliss cou'd keep.
Thus, anxious Thoughts in endless Circles roul,
Without a Centre where to fix the Soul :
In this wilde Maze their vain Endeavours end :
How can the less the Greater comprehend ?
Or finite Reason reach Infinity ?
For what cou'd Fathom God were more than He.

Philip Sydney's poetry being concerned almost exclusively with his love theme, it affords little occasion for our philosophic dogmatism, but in his best poem he expounds his artistic creed with an assurance that invites no dispute :

Loving in truth, and fain in verse my love to show,
That she, dear she, might take some pleasure of my pain,—
Pleasure might cause her read, reading might make her
    know,—
Knowledge might pity win, and pity grace obtain,—
I sought fit words to paint the blackest face of woe ;
Studying inventions fine, her wits to entertain,
Oft turning others' leaves, to see if thence would flow
Some fresh and fruitful showers upon my sunburn'd brain.
But words came halting forth, wanting Invention's stay ;
Invention, Nature's child, fled step-dame Study's blows ;
And others' feet still seem'd but strangers in my way.
Thus, great with child to speak, and helpless in my throes,
Biting my truant pen, beating myself for spite ;
Fool, said my Muse to me, look in thy heart, and write.

Even more passionately Keats moralizes to the same purpose :

A thing of beauty is a joy for ever :
Its loveliness increases ; it will never
Pass into nothingness ; but still will keep
A bower quiet for us, and a sleep
Full of sweet dreams, and health, and quiet breathing.

These are the first lines that he published to the world, and in *Hyperion*, the work of his maturest genius, he was still pressing the argument :

Upon that very hour, our parentage,
The Heavens and the Earth, were manifest :
Then thou first-born, and we the giant-race,
Found ourselves ruling new and beauteous realms.
Now comes the pain of truth, to whom 'tis pain ;
O folly ! for to bear all naked truths,
And to envisage circumstance, all calm,
That is the top of sovereignty.   Mark well !
As Heaven and Earth are fairer, fairer far
Than Chaos and blank Darkness, though once chiefs ;
And as we show beyond that Heaven and Earth
In form and shape compact and beautiful,
In will, in action free, companionship,
And thousand other signs of purer life ;
So on our heels a fresh perfection treads,
A power more strong in beauty, born of us
And fated to excel us, as we pass
In glory that old Darkness : nor are we
Thereby more conquer'd, than by us the rule
Of shapeless Chaos.   Say, doth the dull soil
Quarrel with the proud forests it hath fed,
And feedeth still, more comely than itself ?
Can it deny the chiefdom of green groves ?
Or shall the tree be envious of the dove
Because it cooeth, and hath snowy wings
To wander wherewithal and find its joys ?
We are such forest-trees, and our fair boughs
Have bred forth, not pale solitary doves,
But eagles golden-feather'd, who do tower
Above us in their beauty, and must reign
In right thereof ; for 't is the eternal law
That first in beauty should be first in might :

This, clearly, is doctrine, and Keats at no time had mis-
givings as its missioner :

> O Attic shape ! Fair attitude ! with brede
>   Of marble men and maidens overwrought,
> With forest branches and the trodden weed ;
>   Thou, silent form, dost tease us out of thought
> As doth eternity : Cold Pastoral !
> When old age shall this generation waste,
>   Thou shalt remain, in midst of other woe
> Than ours, a friend to man, to whom thou say'st,
> ' Beauty is truth, truth beauty,'—that is all
>   Ye know on earth, and all ye need to know.

As for Shakespeare, philosophic and moral assertion
are stamped upon his work at large with magnificent
authority. One example will serve :

> Time hath, my lord, a wallet at his back
> Wherein he puts alms for oblivion,
> A great-sized monster of ingratitudes :
> Those scraps are good deeds past ; which are devour'd
> As fast as they are made, forgot as soon
> As done : perseverance, dear my lord,
> Keeps honour bright : to have done, is to hang
> Quite out of fashion, like a rusty mail
> In monumental mockery . . .
> For time is like a fashionable host,
> That slightly shakes his parting guest by the hand ;
> And with his arms outstretch'd, as he would fly,
> Grasps-in the comer : welcome ever smiles,
> And farewell goes out sighing. O, let not virtue seek
> Remuneration for the thing it was,
> For beauty, wit,
> High birth, vigour of bone, desert in service,
> Love, friendship, charity, are subjects all
> To envious and calumniating time.

One touch of nature makes the whole world kin,—
That all, with one consent, praise new-born gawds,
Though they are made and moulded of things past ;
And give to dust, that is a little gilt,
More laud than gilt o'er-dusted.
The present eye praises the present object.

And so one might proceed to compile a substantial
corpus of English poetry in illustration of the text.
A full muster of the poets would be assembled. They
would testify in common with these few whom we
may call. There is Milton, with :

To whom thus also the Angel last replied :
' This having learn'd, thou hast attain'd the sum
Of wisdom ; hope no higher, though all the stars
Thou knew'st by name, and all the ethereal powers,
All secrets of the deep, all Nature's works,
Or works of God, in Heaven, Air, Earth, or Sea,
And all the riches of this world enjoy'dst,
And all the rule, one empire ; only add
Deeds to thy knowledge answerable, add faith,
Add virtue, patience, temperance, add love,
By name to come call'd charity, the soul
Of all the rest ; then wilt thou not be loth
To leave this Paradise, but shalt possess
A Paradise within thee, happier far. . . .
                         . . . go, waken Eve ;
Her also I with gentle dreams have calm'd
Portending good, and all her spirits composed
To meek submission : . . .
That ye may live, which will be many days,
Both in one faith unanimous, though sad
With cause for evils past, yet much more cheer'd
With meditation on the happy end.'

And Wordsworth :

> The world is too much with us ; late and soon,
> Getting and spending, we lay waste our powers :
> Little we see in Nature that is ours ;
> We have given our hearts away, a sordid boon !
> This Sea that bares her bosom to the moon ;
> The winds that will be howling at all hours,
> And are up-gathered now like sleeping flowers ;
> For this, for everything, we are out of tune ;
> It moves us not.—Great God ! I'd rather be
> A Pagan suckled in a creed outworn ;
> So might I, standing on this pleasant lea,
> Have glimpses that would make me less forlorn ;
> Have sight of Proteus rising from the sea ;
> Or hear old Triton blow his wreathèd horn.

And Shelley :

> True love in this differs from gold and clay,
> That to divide is not to take away.
> Love is like understanding, that grows bright,
> Gazing on many truths ; 'tis like thy light,
> Imagination ! which from earth and sky,
> And from the depths of human fantasy,
> As from a thousand prisms and mirrors, fills
> The Universe with glorious beams, and kills
> Error, the worm, with many a sun-like arrow
> Of its reverberated lightning. Narrow
> The heart that loves, the brain that contemplates,
> The life that wears, the spirit that creates
> One object, and one form, and builds thereby
> A sepulchre for its eternity.

> Mind from its object differs most in this :
> Evil from good ; misery from happiness ;
> The baser from the nobler ; the impure
> And frail, from what is clear and must endure.

If you divide suffering and dross, you may
Diminish till it is consumed away ;
If you divide pleasure and love and thought,
Each part exceeds the whole ; and we know not
How much, while any yet remains unshared,
Of pleasure may be gained, or sorrow spared :
This truth is that deep well, whence sages draw
The unenvied light of hope ; the eternal law
By which those live, to whom this world of life
Is as a garden ravaged, and whose strife
Tills for the promise of a later birth
The wilderness of this Elysian earth.

And Tennyson :

How dull it is to pause, to make an end,
To rust unburnish'd, not to shine in use !
As tho' to breathe were life. Life piled on life
Were all too little, and of one to me
Little remains : but every hour is saved
From that eternal silence, something more,
A bringer of new things ; and vile it were
For some three suns to store and hoard myself,
And this grey spirit yearning in desire
To follow knowledge, like a sinking star,
Beyond the utmost bound of human thought.

.   .   .   .   .   .

The lights begin to twinkle from the rocks :
The long day wanes : the slow moon climbs : the deep
Moans round with many voices. Come, my friends,
'Tis not too late to seek a newer world.
Push off, and sitting well in order smite
The sounding furrows ; for my purpose holds
To sail beyond the sunset, and the baths
Of all the western stars, until I die.
It may be that the gulfs will wash us down :
It may be we shall touch the Happy Isles,
And see the great Achilles, whom we knew.

Tho' much is taken, much abides ; and tho'
We are not now that strength which in old days
Moved earth and heaven ; that which we are, we are ;
One equal temper of heroic hearts,
Made weak by time and fate, but strong in will
To strive, to seek, to find, and not to yield.

And Arnold :

O born in days when wits were fresh and clear,
And life ran gaily as the sparkling Thames ;
Before this strange disease of modern life,
With its sick hurry, its divided aims,
Its heads o'ertax'd, its palsied hearts, was rife—
Fly hence, our contact fear !
Still fly, plunge deeper in the bowering wood !
Averse, as Dido did with gesture stern
From her false friend's approach in Hades turn,
Waves us away, and keep thy solitude.

Still nursing the unconquerable hope,
Still clutching the inviolable shade,
With a free onward impulse brushing through,
By night, the silver'd branches of the glade—
Far on the forest skirts, where none pursue,
On some mild pastoral slope
Emerge, and resting on the moonlit pales,
Freshen thy flowers, as in former years,
With dew, or listen with enchanted ears,
From the dark dingles, to the nightingales.

But fly our paths, our feverish contact fly !
For strong the infection of our mental strife,
Which, though it gives no bliss, yet spoils for rest ;
And we should win thee from thy own fair life,
Like us distracted, and like us unblest.
Soon, soon thy cheer would die,

Thy hopes grow timorous, and unfix'd thy powers,
   And thy clear aims be cross and shifting made :
   And then thy glad perennial youth would fade,
Fade, and grow old at last, and die like ours.

And, finally, from our own time, W. B. Yeats :

Now all the truth is out,
Be secret and take defeat
From any brazen throat,
For how can you compete,
Being honour bred, with one
Who were it proved he lies
Were neither shamed in his own
Nor in his neighbours' eyes ;
Bred to a harder thing
Than Triumph, turn away
And like a laughing string
Whereon mad fingers play
Amid a place of stone,
Be secret and exult,
Because of all things known
That is most difficult.

The nature of pure poetry may disregard moral purposes, but the poets have been pertinacious moralists. Philosophic and moral dogmatism has constantly been employed by them as material, and vitally absorbed into the tissue of their work. Critical theory that denies to poetry this dogmatic franchise is opposed by the practice of the poets, and should be discarded.

XII

SOME CONTRIBUTIONS TO THE ENGLISH ANTHOLOGY

(WITH SPECIAL REFERENCE TO THE SEVENTEENTH CENTURY)

WARTON LECTURE ON ENGLISH POETRY

Read February 23, 1922

' HE may at least be sure of a place in the anthologies of the future' is a reviewer's phrase that has brought comfort, I suppose, to a good many poets who have not hoped for the larger things of fame. And yet it is strange, for all the diligence of the compilers, to find how many good poets pass with their death into what it would seem may be, but for some lucky accident, permanent oblivion. Herrick publishes his *Hesperides* in 1648, and no further edition of what is probably the greatest single volume of lyrics in the language is called for until 1810, when John Nott of Bristol, M.D., comes forward with *Select Poems embellished with Occasional Remarks.* Andrew Marvell dies unpublished, but, a little more fortunate in his posthumous fame, appears in a handsome little folio in 1681, which is followed by a new edition forty-five years later, by another fifty years later still, and then he waits nearly another hundred years for the almost universal industry of Dr. Grosart. So good a poet as Richard Corbet, with his *Farewell Rewards and Fairies*, appears first in 1647, then again in a surreptitious edition in 1648, and then for a third time in 1672. In 1807 he is rediscovered by Octavius Gilchrist, and after that he remains unedited until our own time ; while a poet such as Rochester, at his best a lyrist that none of them can surpass, has never from the beginning had his text or his canon rescued from confusion.[1] These poets are among those who, even in long periods of public neglect, have never wholly escaped the attention of scholars or occasional inclusion in the miscellanies, but the absence of any readily accessible editions of their works has meant that over and over again one student or compiler has merely relied for his knowledge or selection upon one or two poems singled out by his predecessors, and this even when the work in hand has been a serious study and not merely a piece of easy book-compiling. The ordinary hack anthologist need not be considered. In nearly every case he simply steals, more or less at haphazard, from the patient labours of honester men than himself. But it is remarkable how, if we take our view of a poet from, say, ten standard English anthologies, we may easily get a hopelessly inadequate view of his work. To take two examples. Richard Barnefield is a name at least known to every reader who is familiar at all with English poetry. His original editions are practically unprocurable, there being in each case perhaps but three or four known copies, while the Roxborough reprint is by no means common, and otherwise the ordinary reader is cut off from access to the full texts. Looking at these ten anthologies, *The*

[1] Since writing this, I am glad to see that Mr. Montagu Summers is engaged on an edition of Rochester.

Golden Treasury, *The Oxford Book of English Verse*, Ward's *English Poets*, Beeching's *Paradise of English Poetry*, Mrs. Meynell's *Flower of the Mind*, Sir Arthur Quiller Couch's *Golden Pomp*, Henley's *English Lyrics*, Mr. Massingham's *Seventeenth Century English Verse*, Mr. Braithwaite's *Elizabethan Verse*, and, last, the frankly popular but very comprehensive *Book of English Poetry* published by Messrs. Jack, we get this result. Mr. Massingham omits Barnefield altogether, as he does not come within his period ; of the other nine, seven give *The Nightingale* alone, while the other two give *The Nightingale* and *If Music and Sweet Poetry Agree*, and Ward adds one other sonnet. This means that to all intents and purposes Barnefield is known to nearly the whole English poetry reading public by one poem, and that, charming as it is, not in my opinion his best. As an example of the quality which is entirely unknown to the general reader, and almost so to the scholar, let me quote two of Barnefield's pieces from *Poems in Divers Humors* published by John Jaggard in 1598 :

AN EPITAPH UPON THE DEATH OF HIS AUNT,
MISTRESSE ELIZABETH SKRYMSHER

Loe here beholde the certaine Ende, of euery liuing wight :
No Creature is secure from Death, for Death will haue his
    Right.
He spareth none : both rich and poore, both young and olde
    must die ;
So fraile is flesh, so short is Life, so sure Mortalitie.
When first the Bodye liues to Life, the soule first dies to
    sinne :
And they that loose this earthly Life, a heavenly Life shall
    winne,
If they liue well : as well she liv'd, that lyeth Vnder heere ;

Whose Vertuous Life to all the Worlde, most plainly did
appeere.
Good to the poore, friend to the rich, and foe to no Degree :
A President of modest Life, and peerelesse Chastitie.
Who louing more, Who more belov'd, of euerie honest
mynde ?
Who more to Hospitalitie, and Clemencie inclinde
Then she ? that being buried here, lyes wrapt in Earth below ;
From whence wee came, to whom wee must, and bee as shee
is now,
A Clodd of Clay : though her pure soule in endlesse Blisse
doeth rest ;
Ioying all Ioy, the Place of Peace, prepared for the blest :
Where holy Angells sit and sing, before the King of Kings ;
Not mynding worldly Vanities, but onely heavenly Things.
Vnto which Ioy, Vnto which Blisse, Vnto which Place of
Pleasure,
God graunt that wee may come at last, t'inioy that heauenly
Treasure.
Which to obtaine, to liue as shee hath done let us endeuor ;
That we may liue with Christ himselfe (above) that liues
for ever.

A COMPARISON OF THE LIFE OF MAN

Mans life is well compared to a feast,
Furnisht with choice of all Varietie :
To it comes Tyme ; and as a bidden guest
Hee sets him downe, in Pompe and Maiestie ;
The three-folde Age of Man, the Waiters bee.
  Then with an earthen voyder (made of clay)
  Comes Death, & takes the table clean away.

My other example is James Shirley. All ten antho-
logists give us *The Glories of our Blood and State*, with
the exception of Mr. Massingham, who omits it on the
plea that it is too well known for inclusion, six add

Victorious Men of Earth No More, four add the hymn
O Fly my Soul, three *You Virgins That Did Late Despair*,
two *The Garden*, while Ward and Mr. Massingham each
add one individual selection.   This means that Shirley's
total representation in ten serious anthologies is by seven
poems, four of which only make seven appearances
between them.   Of these seven poems, four are taken
from the Plays or Masques, and only three, which three
make but six appearances between them, are taken from
Shirley's principal lyric production, the *Poems* of 1646,
a volume of which the future anthologist might take
further notice.   Here is a sombre but finely lyrical
fragment to tempt him :

THE PASSING BELL

Hark, how chimes the Passing bell,
There's no musick to a knell ;
All the other sounds we hear,
Flatter, and but cheat our ear.
This doth put us still in mind
That our flesh must be resign'd,
And a general silence made,
The world be muffled in a shade ;
He that on his pillow lies
Tear-embalmed before he dies,
Carries like a sheep his life,
To meet the sacrificer's knife,
And for eternity is prest,
Sad Bell-weather to the rest.

It is true that in some cases the anthologist could
plead that in following the general choice he was also
representing the poet at his indisputable best.   If we
want to know what, say, Lovelace and Waller were as
poets, we must read *Tell me not, Sweet, I am unkind*,

and *When Love with unconfined Wings,* and *Go lovely Rose,* and it would be an affectation for the compiler to pretend that any other choice could be within reasonable distance of matching these. But with poets like Barnefield and Shirley, and there are many of them, it is another matter. And we find over and over again even first-rate writers whose general reputations rest on two or three well-known pieces because the compilers of anthologies have failed to familiarize themselves with the original sources. And if this is so with poets who, like Shirley, because of the general volume of their work, cannot escape some attention, what is likely to happen to those less fortunate, and doubtless on the whole less admirable ones, who, publishing like Herrick perhaps in 1648, have no Dr. Nott in 1810 nor Dr. Grosart in 1870.

It is as a slight contribution to the answer to this question that the present paper is offered. The history of English poetry, of which, I suppose, the father may be said to be Thomas Warton, is as likely as other histories always to remain incomplete. The explorer of the byways of English verse knows how often he can defeat the indices of even so learned and exhaustive scholars as Doctors Courthope and Saintsbury. This paper makes no pretence to learning of the standard which modern editorship has made prevalent at every seat of learning in the country. The minutiae of research into questions of texts and sources may be said to have become a special profession requiring a most exact and arduous training. That is not my job. I come before you as the most amateur of scholars, but, having all my life read English poetry as widely as I could, I have for some time amused myself by collecting any books of English verse which bore unfamiliar, or, better still, unknown names. In offering a garland from these little books, mostly of the seventeenth century, while I cannot claim that in every case the poet in question is one unknown even to the most diligent student, I am sure that they all have so small a reputation through the body of their work as to amount to nothing at all, and as a group they may be said, with but little exaggeration, to have escaped the anthologists altogether. For some time I had intended to make a small anthology covering this ground myself, but then I realized that for the dozen or twenty discoveries that I might make there were ten times as many that I should miss, and it seemed better in this way to make a few notes in the hope that other readers might from time to time do the same thing, until something really comprehensive in the way of material might be ready for the perfect compiler when he arrives. In most cases these poets are not even known to the historians, and their only monument is inclusion in such publications as the splendid Grolier Club bibliography, mention in which is a guarantee to the bookseller rather than to the critic, although it should be said that though that publication is clearly bibliographical in intention, it had the great advantage of being supervised by Mr. Beverly Chew, who is not only a most distinguished collector but also a man of the finest literary taste and judgement.

With one of my unknown poets, John Collop, I have already dealt at length in a separate paper.[1] He happens to be a poet whose little book, *Poesia Rediviva*, 1656, is of considerable quality throughout, whereas in many cases one finds only a snatch here and there which merits remembrance :

[1] This paper has since been published in a Collection of Essays, *A Book for Bookmen*, Sidgwick & Jackson, 1926.

> The house is swept
> Which sin so long foul kept :
> The peny's found for which the loser wept.
> And purg'd with tears,
> God's Image re-appears.
> The peny truly shews whose stamp it bears.

Collop could write so, and often, but the paper
referred to contains a good many examples of his work,
and he need not be considered further here. I now
propose to present my gatherings with as little in the way
of design as may be found in the occasional note-book.

In 1662 there appeared a volume entitled *Flamma sine
Fumo : or Poems without Fictions*, by R. W., being a
collection of miscellaneous poems including at the end
*A Looking-Glass for the sick, or The Causes of Symptoms
or Signs of Several Diseases with Their Cures and Remedies*,
being the complete physician in amusing doggerel. My
copy of the book from the Huth Library comes from
the Heber Collection and contains a note in Heber's
writing to the effect that R. W., who as we learn from
the signed Preface was Rowland Watkyns, was minister
of Barn in Brecknockshire. He is unknown to Corser,
Collins, and Courthope, but he is to be found in the
Bibliotheca Anglo-Poetica. So far as I can discover,
except for occasional mention in a catalogue, his is to-day
an entirely dead name, and I have discovered no critical
reference to him. Here are a few examples of his work :

THE BIBLE

> Much books I have perus'd, but I protest
> Of books the sacred Bible is the best,
> Some books may much of humane Learning boast
> But here's the Language of the Holy Ghost,
> Hence we draw living water, here we do
> Observe the Patriarchs lives, and doctrine too :

Here Christ himself directs us how to pray,
And to the Gate of Heaven chalks the way.
Here is the salve, which gives the blind their sight,
All darknesse to expel, here is the light :
Here is strong meat for men ; and milk to feed
The weaker babes, which more perfection need ;
Cast off erroneous pamphlets, wanton rhymes,
All feigned books of love ; which cheat the times ;
And read this book of life ; those shall appear
With Christ in Heaven which are written here.

THE WEDDING GARMENT

Faith is the wedding garment, lind within,
With love, without foul spots, or staines of sin.
Humility is the most decent lace,
And patient hope, which doth this garment grace.
Without this royal robe no guest is fit
To sup, or at the Lords own table sit.

THE WISH

Hoc est summum mei, caputque voti.

A little house, a quiet wife,
Sufficient food to nourish life,
Most perfect health, and free from harm,
Convenient cloths to keep me warm.
The liberty of foot, and mind,
And grace the ways of God to find.
This is the summe of my desire,
Until I come unto heavens quire.

UPON THE FAIR AND VERTUOUS GENTLEWOMAN MRS. M. S.
THAT CAN SING EXCELLENTLY

Gratior est virtus veniens è corpore pulchro.

When first I did this Virgin spie,
The object pleas'd my serious eye :
But when I heard her sing, I swear,
The musick took both heart and ear.

Those inward vertues please us best,
Which are with outward beauty drest ;
And 'tis a comely thing to find
In bodies fair, a fairer mind :
The Harp, the Viol hither bring,
And Birds, musitians of the Spring ;
When she doth sing, those must be mute,
They are but Cymbals to the Lute :
She with her Notes doth rise, and fall,
More sweetly than the Nightingal :
God in her pious heart keeps place,
Some Angel in her voice and face.

UPON THE MOST BEAUTIFUL, HOSPITABLE, AND INGENUOUS GENTLEWOMAN MRS. BLANCH MORGAN OF THE THEROW

Some fragrant flowers the smell, some trees the sight
Do much content, some pearls are wondrous bright :
There's not so sweet a flower, so fair a tree,
So pure a gemme in all the world, as she :

Some Ladies humble are, and some are wise ;
Some chast, some kind, some fair to please the eyes ;
All vertues do in her like stars appear,
And make a glorious constellation there.

THE MERCIFUL SAMARITAINE

No balm from Gilead, no Physitian can
Heal me, but Christ the true Samaritan.
When I am sick, and when my wounds are foul,
He hath his oyle and wine to clense my soul.
My sins the thieves, which wounded me, have bin,
Help, Lord, conduct me to thy peaceful Inn.

THE GARDENER

She, supposing him to be the Gardener, said unto him,
John 20.

Mary prevents the day ; she rose to weep,
And see the bed, where Jesus lay asleep.
She found out whom she sought ; but doth not know
Her Masters face ; he is the Gardener now.
This Gardener Edens Garden did compose,
For which the chiefest Plants and Flowers he chose.
He took great care to have sweet Rivers run
T'enrich the ground, where he his work begun.
He is the Gardener still, and knoweth how
To make the Lilies and the Roses grow.
He knows the time to set, when to remove
His living plants to make them better prove.
He hath his pruning knife, when we grow wild,
To tame our nature, and make us more mild :
He curbs his dearest children : when 'tis need,
He cuts his choycest Vine, and makes it bleed.
He weeds the poisonous herbs, which clog the ground.
He knows the rotten hearts, he knows the sound.
The blessed Virgin was the pleasant bower,
This Gardener lodg'd in his appointed hour :
Before his birth his Garden was the womb,
In death he in a Garden chose his Tomb.

PROVERBIAL SENTENCES

Who hath the better game, doth fear the end :
Who hath the worse, doth hope the game may mend.

. . . .

Who in the glass doth oft behold her face,
Hath little care to dress her dwelling place.

. . . . .

When once the tree is fallen, which did stand,
Then every man will take his axe in hand.

   •   •   •   •

No Church yard is so hansome any where,
As will straight move one to be buried there.

   •   •   •   •

Here is great talk of Turk and Pope : but I
Find that my neighbour doth more hurt than they.

A disappointing poet is Robert Wild, whose *Iter Boreale* was first published in 1660. That Wild should have escaped the critics and enthusiasts is not surprising, since as a poet he is continually within a word of an achievement that he as continually misses. I mention him here merely on account of a bibliographical point in connexion with his one lovely moment of inspiration. Mr. Braithwaite, in his *Book of Restoration Verse*, gives his *Epitaph for a Godly Mans Tomb* without any proper indication as to its source, and Mr. Massingham, whose *Seventeenth Century English Verse* is on the whole a very satisfying and original piece of work, gives the same *Epitaph* as coming from the *Iter Boreale* of 1660. In fact it was not in the first edition of 1660 nor the second of 1661 nor the third of 1665, but it made its first appearance in the fourth edition dated 1668. Once elsewhere in a single line,

Newgate or Hell were Heav'n if Christ were there . . .

Wild promises to satisfy expectations. But otherwise it is in the *Epitaph*, and here alone, that he proves himself, for one glorious breath, a poet. I know of hardly any other case of a man courting the muse so constantly with no favour given, and then coming into the full presence for one marvellous moment, to return to the darkness for ever :

AN EPITAPH FOR A GODLY MANS TOMB

Here lies a piece of Christ, a Star in Dust ;
A Vein of Gold, a China Dish that must
Be us'd in Heav'n, when God shall Feast the Just.

Had Wild done any considerable body of work at that
pitch he would have been among the great lyrists.   As
it is he is dust, with his one little jewel to catch the
eye of a very occasional traveller in passing.   His second
best is the not charmless doggerel :

> Alas, poor scholar
> Whither wilt thou go ?

which, however, is of little importance.

Another poet almost, although not entirely, unknown
to the anthologists is Edward Sherburne, whose *Salmacis,
Lyrian and Sylvia, Forsaken Lydia, The Rape of Hellen,
a Comment thereon, with severall other Poems and Trans-
lations*, was published in 1651.   Mr. Braithwaite, whose
anthological range is an unusually wide one, gives seven
of his lyrics, and Mr. Massingham one.   But it remained
for Professor Grierson, in his *Metaphysical Lyrics and
Poems of the Seventeenth Century*, to re-publish the lovely
lyric, *The Proud Aegyptian Queen*.   I may boast to myself
privately that I had the poem in my note-book before
Professor Grierson's book appeared, and he will, I am
sure, not grudge me the pleasure of following him in
drawing attention to his discovery in the hope that
by this Sherburne may find yet two or three more
readers :

AND SHE WASHED HIS FEET WITH HER TEARES, AND WIPED
THEM WITH THE HAIRS OF HER HEAD

The proud Ægyptian Queen, her Roman Guest,
(T'express her Love in Hight of State, and Pleasure)
With Pearl dissolv'd in Gold, did feast,
    Both Food, and Treasure.
And now (dear Lord !) thy Lover, on the fair
And silver Tables of thy Feet, behold !
    Pearl in her Tears, and in her Hair,
        Offers thee Gold.

Another poet who has hitherto received far less atten-
tion than is his due is Thomas Flatman,[1] whose *Poems
and Songs* first appeared in 1674. Quite lately Professor
Saintsbury has given a full edition of his work in the
third volume of his admirable *Caroline Poets*, so that
the fame of

There's an experienc't Rebel, Time,
    And in his Squadrons Poverty ;
There's Age that brings along with him
    A terrible Artillery . . .

and many other such fortunate things can no longer
be said to be in obscurity.

Mathew Stevenson, whose *Occasions Off-spring or
Poems upon Severall Occasions* was published in 1654,
appears, on the other hand, apart from an occasional
bibliographical reference, to have escaped the attention
of anybody at all. His book is pleasant reading always,
and one longish poem, *At the Florists Feast in Norwich*,
is full of colour and delight. It is too long to quote

---

[1] Flatman was, of course, well known to Mr. Bullen. But, then,
what poet was not ?

in full, but here is the concluding Song, which in itself
ought to give Stevenson his place in the collections :

THE SONG

Stay ! O stay ! ye winged howers,
The windes that ransack East, and West,
Have breathd perfumes upon our flowers,
More fragrant then the Phœnix nest :
Then stay ! O stay sweet howers ! that yee,
May witnesse that, which time nere see.

Stay a while, thou featherd Syth-man,
And attend the Queen of flowers,
Show thy self for once a blyth man,
Come dispence with a few howers :
Else we our selves will stay a while,
And make our pastime, Time beguile.

This day is deigned to Floras use,
If yee will revell too, to night
Weel presse the Grape, to lend ye juyce,
Shall make a deluge of delight :
And when yee cant hold up your heads,
Our Garden shall afford ye beds.

A poet even less known than Stevenson, if that were
possible, is Daniel Cudmore, the author of *Ευχοδια or
A Prayer-Song. Being Sacred Poems on The History of
the Birth and Passion of our Blessed Saviour*, published in
1655. His muse is a little laboured, and his lyric flights
generally more notable for length than for certainty
and grace. Nevertheless he sometimes achieves a dark
beauty of his own, as in the following on a text from
Mark :

1

If could some Delius with divided hands
Sound the Seas depth, and on his souls recorder
Imprint the wracks, huge rocks, and heaps of sands,
Which there lie scatter'd in confus'd disorder :
　　This could he do, by Nature's strength or art,
　　Yet none could sound the bottom of the heart.

2

Should some Ship-master make's fore-split the Probe
Of Nature's secrets, and so bring to view
Land to make up a perfect earthly Globe,
Which Drake nor Kit Columbus never knew :
　　Yet, as in the great world, so in his own,
　　He must confess there's yet much land unknown.

3

The heart's a Sea for depth, like Sodom-lake
Dead, thick, and gross ; in it will sink no good :
Th' hearts land's unknown ; wherein what monsters make
Their hides and dens, few yet have understood.
　　The centre may be purest earth ; yet th'heart
　　The bodies centre's the corrupter part.

4

Our heart-strings are the cords of vanity ;
Their caverns are the devil's lurking-holes ;
No fit Triangle for the Trinity ;
An habitation more fit for moles :
　　Their cauls the veils of damn'd Hypocrisie.
　　Thus is sum'd up man's wretched Majestie.

5

If thus the Sun within our firmament
Into a Meteor degenerate ;
If thus the King within our continent
Let's sin and lust usurp his Royal state :
    If thus corrupted be the bodies leaven,
    How shall we manchets be prepar'd for heaven ?

6

Whe'er Hell be in th'earth's centre, I suspend ;
But in man's centre's couch'd an Hell of sin :
Nor do so many lines to th' centre tend,
As in a wicked heart fiends make their Inne :
    Which yet most know no more, then can be found
    Where Arethusa windes beneath the ground.

7

Lord, shew me in the Mirrour of thy Law
The horrour of my heart by bright reflection :
In that thy Glass, there falshood is nor flaw :
Though wickedly some scorn its true direction,
    And whip the Tutor for his discipline ;
    Yet Lord direct me by that Glass of thine.

8

Oh daign my heart with graces to perfume,
And th'rowly purge it from each noisome vapor,
Whose rank infection choaks each neighb'ring room,
And strives to damp my soul's aspiring tapor.
    O make my heart-strings, Lord, thy cords of love ;
    So mine according to thy heart shall prove.

In 1638 was published *Kalendarium Humanae Vitae.*
The Kalender of Mans Life. The volume is a charmingly

produced one, embellished with wood-cuts, and consists of reflective poems on the changes of the year, done in both Latin and English verse. The author was Robert Farley, again a poet to-day wholly unknown to fame beyond a collector's note here and there. The following Spring piece, reminiscent in its verse of the poet of *Everyman*, called *Aprill, or Mans Infancie*, is an example of many that should have brought him better luck :

> Thine Infant (Lord) to be I crave,
> Let not my gray hairs sinne to grave.
> My soule doth cry, still thou it Lord
> With milke of thy eternall Word ;
> Author of grace, nurse grace in me,
> So I at length shall strengthened be.
> Clense me from first and second guilt,
> Onely thou canst (Lord) if thou wilt ;
> Then shall I be a Dennizon
> There, where uncleannesse commeth none.
> Let not Hells Siren lull asleepe
> My soule to drowne it in the deepe ;
> Lord make it watch for Heav'ns joyes
> Regarding nothing worldly toyes.
> Behold my soule rock't too and fro,
> Doth cry for feare and cannot goe ;
> Now least in storme it drowned be,
> Take it into the ship with Thee.
> So shall Thou thinke me to be thine,
> And I shall thinke thy kingdome mine ;
> So shall my soule thy mercies prove
> And learne thy mercies how to love.

Mr. Braithwaite and Mr. Massingham give examples, the former three, the latter one, of John Hall, whose *Poems* was published at Cambridge in 1646, and reprinted in *Caroline Poets.* Both these editors give what is perhaps on the whole his best poem, *The Call*, but Mr. Braithwaite's other selections are not, I think, the best that could be made. Otherwise I do not find him quoted anywhere, although here, as in other cases, I am naturally prepared to find that in the great field of poetical research references have escaped me. In any case, Hall, like most of these poets, has only been discovered in these two hundred years by lucky accident or the rarest erudition such as Professor Saintsbury's. His work is full of charming touches, although he seldom brings off a poem completely. This opening of *The Christall*, for example, is a lovely but unfulfilled promise :

> This Christall here
> That shines so clear,
> And carri's in its womb a little day ;
> Once hammerd will appear
> Impure as dust, as dark as clay.

When, however, our perfect anthology is compiled, this little book will have to be examined carefully, as the following example will show :

HOME TRAVELL

> What need I travell, since I may
> More choiser wonders here survay ?
> What need I Tire for purple seek
> When I may find it in a cheek ?
> Or sack the Eastern shores, there lies
> More precious Diamonds in her eyes ?
> What need I dig Peru for Oare
> When every hair of her yields more ?
> Or toile for Gummes in India
> Since she can breath more rich then they ?
> Or ransack Africk, there will be
> On either hand more Ivory ?

But look within, all Vertues that
Each nation would appropriate,
And with the glory of them rest,
Are in this map at large exprest ;
That who would travell here might know
The little world in Folio.

There are not only poets whose claim to some brief attention rests on a stray lyric or two, but even the more difficult cases of men whose good things, even in short poems, lie surrounded by mediocrity. Alexander Ross, for example, whose *Mel Heliconium : or, Poeticall Honey, gathered out of the weeds of Parnassus,* published in 1642, will, I think, yield no completely satisfactory poem to the most diligent search, can yet not infrequently set all our expectations agog by such felicities as

We're all in Atalanta's case,
We run apace,
Untill our wandring eyes behold
The glitt'ring gold :
And then we lose in vanity
Our race, and our virginity. . . .

and

Who glory in your golden hair,
And in smooth Alabaster skins ;
And think with Swans you may compare
In whitenesse, that your cheeks and chins
Can match white Lillies, and
Vermilion.
Yet think upon
The flower that's in your hand.

Again, to turn to our perfect anthology, this particular problem will be greatly intensified for the compiler when he passes beyond the seventeenth into the eighteenth

century, that long, smooth, poetical waste-land in which
lie hidden all sorts of treasures for the finding, apart
from the few that have already become common pro-
perty.   So early as 1692 we have a little volume, *Poems
on Several Occasions*, by Thomas Fletcher, written, as
the author's Preface informs us, when the author was
hardly out of his 'teens, and for the most part without
any merit but that of a common precocity.   But sud-
denly in the middle of the book we come across *Content,
A Pastoral Dialogue*, with passages as good as this :

> *Damon.*   Some wish, and see their Flocks increase ;
> They gain Wealth, but lose their Peace :
> Folds enlarg'd enlarge their Care ;
> Who have much, for much must fear :
> Others see their Flocks decay ;
> With their Flocks they pine away.
> The Shepherd, who would happy be,
> Must not seek Causes for his Joy ;
> Must not for Pretences tarry :
> But be unreasonably merry.
>
> .   .   .   .
>
> If tuneful Birds salute the Spring,
> From the Birds I learn to sing ;
> If the Heavens laugh a while,
> From the Heav'ns I learn to smile :
> But if Mists obscure the Day,
> And black Clouds fright the Sun away ;
> I never dread the angry Sky ;
> Why should I think it frowns on me ?
>
> .   .   .   .
>
> [I]
> Think on the Time, when I shall be
> From Clouds and Storms for ever free ;
> Plac'd in Elysium ; where, they say,
> Blest Ghosts enjoy Eternal Day,

Eternal Spring ; where, all the year,
The Fields their freshest Honours wear.

.   .   .   .   .

In vain the sullen Heavens scowl,
Storms and Tempest round me howl ;
I make fair Weather in my Soul.

Before ending this momentary digression into a later
age, I should like to quote two trifles from another of
the innumerable *Poems on Severall Occasions*, this time
published in 1735, the author John Hughes, the friend
of Addison and Steele, and the dramatist of *The Siege
of Damascus*, a very far from negligible play :

SONNET

(From the French)

I die with too transporting Joy,
    If she I love rewards my Fire ;
If She's inexorably Coy,
    With too much Passion I expire.

No Way the Fates afford to shun
    The cruel Torment I endure ;
Since I am doom'd to be undone
    By the Disease, or by the Cure.

SONG

THE FAIR TRAVELLER

In young Astrea's sparkling Eye,
Resistless Love has fix'd his Throne ;
A thousand Lovers bleeding lie
For Her, with Wounds they fear to own.
While the coy Beauty speeds her Flight
To distant Groves from whence she came ;
So Lightning vanishes from Sight,
But leaves the Forest in a Flame !

Here is at least an elegance which we might expect from a writer who tells us in one of his Essays that ' A plain unletter'd man is always more agreeable Company, than a Fool in several Languages '.

I may, perhaps, here ask a question in the hope that some eighteenth-century expert may be able to throw light on a curious little textual problem. Locker-Lampson in his *Lyra Elegantiarum* gives this lovely lyric :

THE WHITE ROSE

Sent by a Yorkist Gentleman to his Lancastrian Mistress.

> If this fair rose offend thy sight,
>   Placed in thy bosom bare,
> 'Twill blush to find itself less white,
>   And turn Lancastrian there.
>
> But if thy ruby lip it spy,—
>   As kiss it thou mayst deign,—
> With envy pale 'twill lose its dye,
>   And Yorkist turn again.

Locker-Lampson strangely ascribes this to James Somerville, whose dates he gives as 1692 to 1742. There seems to be no authority for bringing such a James Somerville into being, and there is no doubt that William Somervile, 1677, or thereabouts, to 1742, is meant. And, in fact, in *Occasional Poems*, published in 1727, by the author of *The Chase*, there is a poem entitled *Presenting to a Lady a White Rose and a Red, on the Tenth of June*, five stanzas in length, the last three of which are poor, with this opening :

> If this pale rose offend your Sight,
>   It in your bosom wear ;
> 'Twill blush to find itself less white,
>   And turn Lancastrian there.

15

But, Celia, should the Red be chose,
　With gay Vermilion bright ;
'Twou'd sicken at each Blush that glows,
　And in Despair turn White.

One almost wants to make a composite of the two
versions, and it would be interesting to know Locker-
Lampson's authority for his text. He makes no refer-
ence to the poem in his notes. Before leaving Somervile
I should like to give this jest from his Moral Fables :

THE MORAL TO A FABLE, ' THE OYSTER '

Ye men of Norfolk, and of Wales,
　From this learn common Sense ;
Nor thrust your Neighbours into Jayls,
　For ev'ry slight Offence.

Banish those Vermin of Debate,
　That on your Substance feed ;
The Knaves who now are serv'd in Plate,
　Wou'd starve, if Fools agreed.

In addition to the acknowledged and original work
of these poets, and many like them, there are the im-
mense fields of the Translations and the poetical Miscel-
lanies in which to go treasure-hunting. The Miscellanies
themselves still offer wide and profitable opportunity
for research. Mr. Bullen and others have done much,
but there are still volumes, such as one which I have
in my possession, called *New Court Songs and Poems*, by
R. V. Gent, who is supposed by the cataloguers to be
Robert Veele, which are full of delights and riddles.
I am approaching the end of my allotted time, and, in
any case, I should be very hesitant to venture into these
very tricksy regions of speculation. Each of us, as we
follow our own reading, may make a lucky attribution

here and there, but to sort any of these volumes out into clear order would need qualifications not mine. Mere guess-work brings no enlightenment with it, and to indulge in it would mean that one could only approach one's audience something in the mood of the Printer of Richard Fanshawe's *Il Pastor Fido* in the second issue of 1648, who addressed his reader thus :

Reader,

Thou wilt meet in the Additionall Poems with many literall Errours, and in Pastor Fido with some, besides the two noted at the end thereof. It will be easie for Thee, with thy judgment and good heed to rectifie all as thou goest along. I beseech thee doe it to salve my credit with him that set me a work. Who am of Those that had rather confesse their faults, than mend them.

Farewell.

In reading through such poems as these that have been here considered, one is struck anew with the immense wisdom of Wordsworth's remark that ' Poetry is emotion recollected in tranquillity '. These poets, we may be sure, were most of them passionate, heady people, troubled and shaken by life and their own character. And yet in reading through their verses all the smother has gone, and we move through clear and tranquil, but none the less exhilarating, airs. Indeed it is this kind of tranquillity which is the most bracing of all conditions. Here is to be found the true balance of form. As William Habington, the poet of *Castara*, said :

He hath by a liberall education beene softned to civility ; for that rugged honesty some rude men professe, is an indigested Chaos ; which may containe the seedes of goodnesse, but it wants forme and order.

And by way of Habington we may, before closing,

make a brief return to the seventeenth century, which has been chiefly our concern. Habington, on the whole, has been dealt fairly with by the anthologists, but his book contains many pieces worth remembering besides *Ye blushing Virgins happy are*, and *When I Survey the bright Celestial Sphere*, by which he is usually represented ; this, for example, *Upon the Thought of Age and Death*, which I take from the third edition of 1639, as having at one point a better text than the first edition of 1634 :

> The breath of time shall blast the flowry Spring,
> Which so perfumes thy cheeke, and with it bring
> So darke a mist, as shall eclipse the light
> Of thy faire eyes, in an eternall night.
> Some melancholly chamber of the earth,
> (For that like Time devoures whom it gave breath)
> Thy beauties shall entombe, while all who ere
> Lov'd nobly, offer up their sorrowes there.
> But I whose griefe no formall limits bound,
> Beholding the darke caverne of that ground,
> Will there immure myselfe. And thus I shall
> Thy mourner be, and my owne funerall.
>   Else by the weeping magicke of my verse,
>   Thou hadst reviv'd to triumph o're thy hearse.

In conclusion, a word of Joshua Sylvester, known to fame, that strange public that so often reads so little, as the translator of Du Bartas. He appears in a great number of anthologies with the lovely Sonnet *Were I as base as is the lowly plain*, the original appearance of which I have been unable to trace in any of his books that have been accessible to me. Otherwise he has, I think, not been called upon by the compilers at all. And yet there is a very attractive fat little volume, or rather volumes, since a small group of these are nearly always found together, of which the chief titles are *The*

Parliament of Vertues Royal, and *The Second Session of the Parliament of Vertues Reall.* There is no date on either of the title-pages, but from dates on some of the sub-titles it appears to have been published less than ten years, in any case, before Sylvester's death in 1618. Over and over again the poet catches the great note of a great age, as in—

> I cannot strike Appollo's string,
> Study for Heav'n and timely ring
> Sacred Aaron's golden Bell;
> Nor sing at once the Thespian Songs,
> And serve my Country, as belongs:
> Therefore, Muses, heere Fare-well.

The best poem in the book is *Memorials of Mortalitie,* a long and sustained meditation full of brave music. It is in this poem that there is a line, 'Ther's but a Sigh from Table to the Tombe', which anticipates the most famous of Orinda's verses:

> Yet carelessly we run our race,
> As if we could Death's summons waive;
> And think not on the narrow space
> Between the Table and the Grave.

These are a few of the two hundred stanzas of the Memorials:

> Who feares this Death, is more then deadly sick;
> In midst of Life he seems even dead for dreed;
> Death in his brest he beares, as buried Quick:
> For, feare of Death is worse then Death indeed.
>
> .   .   .   .
>
> The World's a Sea, the Galley is this Life,
> The Master, Time; the Pole, Hope promiseth;
> Fortune the Winde; the stormie Tempest, Strife;
> And Man the Rowe-Slave, to the Part of Death.
>
> .   .   .   .

The World is much of a faire Mistress mood,
Which, wilie, makes more Fooles then Favorites;
Hugs These, hates Those; yet will of all be woo'd:
But never keeps the Promise that she plights.

. . . .

Where are Those Monarchs, mighty Conquerors,
Whose brows ere-while the whol Worlds Laurel drest,
When Sea and Land could show no Land but Theirs?
Now, of it All, only Seaven Hils do rest.

. . . .

All These huge Buildings, These proud Piles (alas!)
Which seem'd to threaten, Heav'n it selfe to scale;
Have now given place to Forests, Groves, and Grass;
And Time hath chang'd their Names and Place withall.

. . . .

Thy Term expir'd, Thou put'st-off Payment yet.
And weenst to win much by some Months delay.
Sith pay thou must, wer't not as good be quit?
For, Death will be no gentler any Day.

. . . .

Life, to the life, The Chesse-board lineats;
Where Pawnes and Kings have equall Portion:
This leaps, that limps, this cheks, that neks, that mates
Their Names are diverse; but, their Wood is one.

. . . .

Tis better fall, then stil to feare a Fall:
Tis better die, then to be still a-dying:
The End of Pain ends the Complaint withall:
And nothing grieves that comes but once, and flying.

. . . .

This Life's a Web, woven fine for som, som grosse;
Some Hemp, some Flax, some longer, shorter some;
Good and Ill Haps are but the Threeds acrosse:
And first or last, Death cuts it from the Loom.